**THE INSPIRATIONAL
BEST-SELLING BOOK**

Practical and inspirational insights
for **ANYONE** aged 9 to 90

INSPIRE ME

Life Wisdom To Pass On

SHANE CRADOCK

Published in the United States by Ivory Publishing.

Originally published in paperback in 2010.

Website: www.shanecradock.com

ISBN-13: 978-1788087094
ISBN-10: 1788087094

First Printing November 2010
Book design by Debbie Bishop
Cover design by Debbie Bishop

Second Paperback Edition

Printed in the USA

INSPIRE ME

CONTENTS

Foreword i

Acknowledgements vii

Introduction x

Chapter 1   Your Life, Your Potential....................1

Chapter 2   Using Your Mind............................. 23

Chapter 3   Advice from Greats 44

Chapter 4   Making Friends Effortlessly 66

Chapter 5   The Art Of Communication 88

Chapter 6   Achieving Your Dreams 110

Chapter 7   Being Successful & Happy 132

Chapter 8   Your Good Health 154

Chapter 9   Love and Relationships 176

Chapter 10   Money and Wealth 198

Chapter 11   Succeeding at Business 220

Chapter 12   When Things Go Wrong. 242

Chapter 13   Overcoming Your Fears 264

Chapter 14   The BIGGER Picture
             ...Making A Difference 286

Chapter 15   Living Life On Your Terms 306

INSPIRE ME

For Jane and Sam,

May you live happy lives

that inspire others

FOREWORD

This is not just a book of quotes. That was my first lesson in clarifying when asked what the book was about - when Inspire Me was first published in 2011.

Really it's a book of stories, insights and real life experiences that all have one thing in common - to inspire you.

But as you'll see, each one of those has a quote to anchor the wisdom within.

The idea for this book was born from a weekly email I created in 2008 (with the same title) and it still goes out to thousands of people around the world every Monday. (That still amazes me!)

The regular positive feedback, comments and suggestions from that email gave me the encouragement to write a book under the same name.

So in early 2011, 'Inspire Me - Life Wisdom To Pass On' was published and despite being told by many that 'it wouldn't work', it has gone on to surprise me even more - achieving best-seller status in my home country of Ireland.

Creating this book was a very personal project, not least for the fact that it caused me to reveal a more vulnerable side of my own life story.

What's very satisfying is hearing back from readers some of the actions it has inspired. Here are some:

- An entrepreneur who still gives the book to his clients and team as a 'thank you' - his way of encouraging them to 'keep going for it'.

- A mother who reads from the book to her 9 year old daughter so that she lays the seeds for strong self-belief.

- A man who had given up on his dream of being a full-time writer, until he read one page in 'Inspire Me' and re-committed to his dream.

- A teacher who reads daily from the book to inspire his students to 'Think Big'. And then convinced his principal to read an inspirational quote over the school intercom daily as a result.

- A loving daughter who read from the book daily, to her dying mother, as a comfort in her last days.

- Dental, Doctor and Physiotherapist clinics that keeps having to replace their copy because their patients keep taking it!

I have designed this book in a way that allows you to read it whatever way you want. From cover to cover or random dip in. Each insight is designed to be read very quickly, and usually includes a call to some form of action. And that's the most important thing to remember while reading this book - the best result for you is to be inspired to take action. Otherwise nothing really changes.

I'd also like to add something to this edition of the book that I completely forgot in the original - my appreciation to Robin Sharma, the author of the international best-selling book *'The Monk Who Sold His Ferrari'*.

I met Robin in 2010 after a talk he'd given in Dublin and I asked him for his advice with this book, because it had been rejected by many publishers. He went on to tell me that his own book had also been rejected by publishers and he'd actually given up.

But his Dad encouraged him to self-publish and gave him the money to do a small print run. He sold the book as best he could at events but it was in small quantities. Months later, he ended up chatting with a gentleman in a line in a coffee shop, I think in Toronto, who'd been intrigued by the title of the book he was carrying.

Robin, being the generous soul, that he is, gave the man his book. A few weeks later, that same man rang Robin and told him that he was a senior executive in a top publishing house in North America. He went on to say that he loved the book and wanted to do a deal to take it international. Now, as Robin said to me, this is a one in a million event. The equivalent to getting the Willy Wonka golden ticket!

'But...', he said, 'If I hadn't listened to my Dad and self-published it would never have happened.

So my advice to you Shane, is to just get it out there. You'll be surprised at what the book will bring you.'

It was super advice. So I did what he did and self-published. I will admit that I'm still waiting for someone to tap me on the shoulder in a coffee shop…:), but it has been incredible what has come from 'just getting it out there.'

Clients, speaking engagements, contracts and connections with amazing people all over the world I would never have met otherwise.

And best of all is the knowledge that it continues to make a positive difference to thousands of people all over the world. That is very humbling.

I hope that by sharing that story it inspires you also. Maybe it's time to get your book done? Or just get 'that' project out there. If you do, please let me know.

I always imagined people having this book in their homes, offices and their bags and every now and then they'd go to it for inspiration or encouragement.

Whether you're a business leader, a parent, a student, a sportsperson or someone looking to enjoy your life to the full, the right words have never been more important.

A quote attributed to Benjamin Franklin is:

> *"Life's tragedy is that we get old too soon, and wise too late."*

The purpose of this book is to help you accelerate your wisdom.

My intention is that you enjoy it and that it genuinely inspires you.

Life is precious.

Make it count.

Best,

Shane

January 2017

ACKNOWLEDGEMENTS

Firstly, I'd like to acknowledge my mother for giving me the idea to start recording quotes that inspired me.   If that hadn't happened, this book wouldn't be in your hands.

Thanks also to those who kept encouraging me to get the book out there. Writing the book was one thing. Getting it published proved a bit trickier! So thanks to you anyone who told me to keep going and in particular Tina Fearon, Keelan Cunningham, Declan Connolly, Noreen Farrell, Cathy O'Connor, Sean O'Leary, Niall Wogan, Philip McKernan, Lisa Rushmere, Jeremy Massey and Don Mullan.

Thanks also has to go out to all of the readers of my weekly email at www.shanecradock.com

Your comments, feedback and appreciation gave

me a strong signal that there was a market for a book like this. It certainly helped with the final push!

I wouldn't be able to write a lot of what I do and have the time to work on projects like this unless I had the support of an amazing woman – so Judy, thank you for everything you do. It makes my life a lot easier and I appreciate everything you do for myself, Sam and Jane.

This book was born from years spent collecting thousands of quotes. That all started after a very difficult time in my life. Four people were key in helping me then – Maurice Quinlan, Margaret O'Sullivan and my parents, Jim and Mary.

Words aren't sufficient for what you did for me. I am eternally grateful.

Finally, the last 5% of any project is usually the hardest. The person responsible for that part of this project was Rachel Taglienti. Thanks for all your help with this Rachel – it wouldn't have happened without you.

INTRODUCTION

The acorn for this book was a simple gift my mother gave me at the darkest time in my life. It proved to make a massive difference, particularly whenever dark clouds appeared on the horizon.

The gift was very simple.

A black hard backed lined copy book, full of blank pages.   Seeing the puzzled look on my face when she gave it, my mother guided me to the 1st page. On it she had written the following words,

> *"If you cannot find life's roses,*
> *Go find the daisies sweet*
> *And revel in the common grass*
> *That sparkles at your feet."*

She added,

'Because the simplest words can make such a difference, it's probably a good idea to record the ones that mean the most to you. That way you can read them when you want to be inspired.'
20 years on, and I still have that book, now full of inspiring, thought provoking words.   Not only that, my records have now expanded to my lap-top where I have thousands of quotes stored.

But this book is not a book of quotes.

It's really a book of wisdom, packed with great insights on how to live a successful life.

I've found from experience that it's one thing to read a quote and think 'that's interesting' and it's another thing to REALLY think about HOW TO USE the wisdom of the quote in your life.

With each nugget of information, there is a quote to emphasize the point that is being made. To really make it stick.

There are hundreds of books that can help you live
a better life, but there are few books that have so
much useful information that cover so many different
areas.

Best of all, each chapter is designed to be read very
quickly and is short and sweet. Or you can just pick
it up and see what page randomly opens for you –
very often you can get the message that's directly
relevant to you at that time.

It's my wish that this book inspires you in whatever
way you need and that the words within it really
make a difference to your life. Who knows, in time
maybe you'll even start recording quotes that inspire
you?

Whatever you do, I wish you a successful life, on
your terms.

INSPIRE ME

CHAPTER 1

YOUR LIFE, YOUR POTENTIAL

You are spirit   3

Explore your potential   5

Your life's purpose   7

Live your dreams   9

Your mind is your best asset   11

Achieving the impossible.   13

Develop the best habits   15

Look inside for the answers   17

Be the best you can be   19

Perfect the Art of Living   21

*"We are not physical beings
on a spiritual journey but
spiritual beings
on a physical journey."*

Stephen Covey
Author of
'The Seven Habits of Highly Effective People'

You Are Spirit

There is something more to you than your body.
At some level you know it. And this part of you, no
matter whether it's called your spirit, your soul, your
inner you…

This part of you is the real you.

You can gain all the riches in the world, but if you're
not in tune with your inner spirit, there will be a
complete lack of fulfilment. And this happens a lot.
People achieve the success they always wanted but
often they feel empty.

Your body needs to be fed to survive. If you take
away food, eventually your body will stop. Your
spirit never stops working but its strength and
vibrancy needs nourishment to thrive.

The food that works best are usually things that
don't cost money. A walk in nature. Slowing down
to appreciate what's around you. Taking time to be
quiet. Using your talents to serve others in some
way. Enjoy the world. Just remember, when you
prioritise your spirit, everything works in harmony.

"People travel to wonder at the height of the mountains, at the huge waves of the seas, at the long course of the rivers, at the vast compass of the ocean, at the circular motion of the stars, and yet they pass by themselves without wondering."

St. Augustine of Hippo

EXPLORE OUR POTENTIAL

I have a few friends that love to travel. In fact they're obsessed with it! Seeing new places and experiencing new cultures is very exciting and fun. But most people never think about the amazing unexplored territory that is themselves. They never think of the amazing power they have within.

I remember when a friend travelled the world for a year. She had a great time and the year flew by. When she returned back home to the 'real world', she ended up getting very depressed.

Why? Because life had lost its excitement, it's sense of adventure. Like many others, she was fooled into thinking that a great life depends on where you are. It doesn't.

A great life starts inside you. It starts by discovering who you are. Your talents, your passions, your interests and engaging these to make a positive difference in the world.

That's when the real fun starts…

"To be yourself in a world that is constantly trying to make you something else is the greatest accomplishment."

Ralph Waldo Emerson

1803-1882, American Author, Poet Philosopher

YOUR LIFE'S PURPOSE

Now, this may come as a surprise to you, but we in the Western World are conditioned into being someone we're not.

We're conditioned by the expectations of our parents, friends, families and work colleagues. Magazines, movies and TV shows tell us what we have to have to be 'successful'.

But get this. 'Success' is whatever you decide it to be. And because there is no-one else like you on the planet, it will be unique to you. Many people get caught up in the 'I have to have that' because someone else does. That is the route to unhappiness and dissatisfaction.

Decide what success means to you. Write it down. Just ask yourself why you want it, and if it will really make you happy. Don't expect everyone to agree with you, but if you stick to who you are and are 100% honest with yourself and others, then you will enjoy a success that is very sweet.

"Go confidently in the

direction of your dreams!

Live the life you've imagined.

As you simplify your life,

the laws of the universe

will be simpler."

Henry David Thoreau

1817-1862, American author,
naturalist and philosopher

LIVE YOUR DREAMS

Something pretty cool is happening.

Around the world, more and more people are starting to realise that they can achieve the lives they really want.

As soon as you make a <u>decision</u> to move in the direction of your ideal life, unforeseen things start to kick in to help you on your way. You'll meet people who will help you, circumstances will go your way and luck will be on your side. It's weird but it's true!

But the foundation to all of this is confidently going after your dreams as if you really expect them to happen. The enemy of it is fear and doubt.

Start writing down now what your ideal life would look like, as if it's already happened. Revisit it regularly, and change it as you change.

Over time, something remarkable happens. The life you dreamed of starts appearing.

"A mind that is stretched to a new idea never returns to its original dimension."

Oliver Wendell Holmes

1809-1894, One of the best regarded
American poets of the 19th century

Your Mind Is Your Best Asset

Scientists now acknowledge that the potential of the human mind is unlimited.

The majority of people are only using a tiny fraction of their potential and there is no doubt that the key to accessing more of that potential lies in understanding and making use of the power of your mind.

The top achievers in every field, whether it be sport, business, creativity (or even relationships) all use their minds in a certain way.

Make it a top priority in your life to find out how your mind works and then discipline yourself to make use of it. If you can do this, you will increase the level of joy and fulfilment in your life.

PS – To get you started, there are some tips in the chapter on the mind. We live in a time where we have unlimited access to great teachers in this area. Once you make the decision to explore this subject, they will come to your attention.

"The young do not know enough to be prudent, and therefore they attempt the impossible - and achieve it, generation after generation."

Pearl S. Buck

1892-1973, Prolific writer,
Nobel and Pulitzer Prize Winner

ACHIEVING THE 'IMPOSSIBLE'

At one time, there was no such thing as an aeroplane, a TV, a mobile phone, a computer, the internet, Google…

At one time, all of these would have been considered impossible, yet now we take them totally for granted. This seems to be the way of the world. To laugh at the impossible, and then accept it years later…

This quote reminds us that young people very often get great things done just by trying. They don't know any reason not to succeed and so give it a go.

But there are also many young people who don't give it a go. The trait that makes the difference is one that can exist at any age, if you protect it. What is it? A 'can do' attitude. Saying 'why not?' more than you say 'why?'

As the saying goes, 'Everything is possible. The impossible just takes a bit longer.'

"You are what you

repeatedly do.

Excellence is not an event -

it is a habit"

Aristotle

384-322 BC,

Ancient Greek smart guy.
He taught Alexander The Great.

DEVELOP THE BEST HABITS

As much as 99% of what we do is estimated to be controlled by our unconscious mind, the home of our habits. So it makes sense to cultivate habits that lead us in the direction of our dreams.

The more often you do something, the more likely you are to do it. This is because when you repeat something often, you create an automatic habit in yourself.

So pick a habit you want to have and start. Then keep doing it. At first it will be uncomfortable but as you keep doing it, it will get easier and much more comfortable. And much easier.

So it you want to write, then write. If you want to learn public speaking, then speak! Just start and keep going.

What most people don't see in 'successful' people are the hours, dedication and discipline they have committed to doing the things most people <u>don't like to do.</u>

Ask Jack Nicklaus if he practices much...

*"Your vision will become clear
only when you can look into
your own heart.
Who looks outside, dreams;
who looks inside, awakes."*

Carl Jung

1875-1961, Famous psychologist

LOOK INSIDE FOR THE ANSWERS

A woman met with me once because she had a problem she couldn't solve.

She had everything she ever wanted materially but she realised when she got it all, it really wasn't what she wanted at all! She had lots of money, an amazing car, a wonderful house and lots of other great things in her life but she was unhappy, had poor health and longed for a close relationship.

But most of all, she was out of touch with her 'self'. She was out of touch with who she really was and what she really wanted.

The only tried and tested way of getting in touch with who you are and what you really want is to take time to tune out the world, and to tune into your 'self'.

What happened to the woman? She started to reflect on her life, to relax daily and to spend more time with her 'self' – me time. As she continued doing this she started to see life differently and naturally started to change her priorities. She still has the nice car and house but today she is much happier, healthier and fulfilled.

"Our deepest fear is not that we are inadequate. Our deepest fear is that we are powerful beyond measure. It is our light, not our darkness, that most frightens us. We ask ourselves, who am I to be brilliant, gorgeous, talented and fabulous?

Actually, who are you not to be?

You are a child of God. Your playing small doesn't serve the world. There is nothing enlightened about shrinking so that other people won't feel insecure around you. We were born to make manifest the glory of God that is within us.

It's not just in some of us, it's in everyone. And as we let our own light shine, we unconsciously give other people permission to do the same.

As we are liberated from our own fear, our presence automatically liberates others."

Written by Marianne Williamson and used by Nelson Mandela in his 1994 Inaugural Speech

BE THE BEST
YOU CAN BE

Digest the words on the opposite page.

Maybe even learn it off by heart.

You are completely unique.

Excel at being you.

Be proud of it.

"I am an artist at living –

my work of art is my life."

Suzuki

As in the man with the

cars and motorbikes!

PERFECT THE ART OF LIVING.

There is no doubt but the most worthwhile art to master in your life is the art of living.

How to live a successful life that is a life of love, contribution, wealth, great health, fantastic relationships and fun is something that most people think is outside their reach.

But there are people doing it despite their circumstances.

And if one can do it, all can do it.

Learn from those that excel in certain areas. Figure out their formula. And go for the best in every area of your life.

Your life should be your life's work. Insist on having a great one. And help others to do the same. Now that's a life worth living!

CHAPTER 2

USING YOUR MIND

The best kept secret in the universe

25

Your mind is a creative tool

27

The key to success

29

How 'Super Achievers' think

31

The tools of your mind

33

This determines your life

35

Practice the art of mental relaxation

37

Protect your 'night club'

39

Your state of mind

41

Get out of the way of the power

43

*"The greatest undeveloped
territory in the world lies
under your hat"*

Anonymous

THE BEST KEPT SECRET IN THE UNIVERSE

Your mind is an amazing tool. Realise that apart from nature, everything that exists in the world now, was at one point only an idea. But through persistence and the right use of their minds, people just like you and I brought these ideas into 'reality.' But some people seem to be better at doing this than others and it's likely they are not aware of the role their mind played in their achievements.

And if you aren't aware of it or know it's power, then how can you expect to take full advantage of it? It'd be like having a super charged Ferrari in your garage and not knowing!

Step 1: Realise the power of your mind.
Step 2: Find out how to use it to your advantage.
Step 3: Put your knowledge into action!

Your life is a result of how well you can harness the power of your mind. Most people go through their lives without realising the power they're carrying between their two ears.

Make it your business to activate your mind's potential. How? For starters, read on!

"The man who has no imagination has no wings."

Muhammad Ali

Your Mind Is A Creative Tool.

The great thinkers throughout time recognised the power of your mind to create.

It has such awesome power that it can create a heaven or a hell, depending on how you use it. And history has shown that regardless of your 'apparent' limitations, human beings can achieve the impossible, if they allow themselves to dream it.

Your mind is an amazing tool of creativity and can be used for the benefit of the world or the destruction of life. It's your choice. Where do you start? Well, firstly, realise that your imagination has immense power.

Your mind helps you create what you want in your life. If you wish to bring something into your life that doesn't exist, the starting point is to imagine it in your mind. That's the first step. The second is to believe you can bring it into reality and the third is to stick with it until you get it.

The believing is the most important, and it all starts with what you imagine in your mind...

"Whatever the mind

can conceive and believe

it will achieve."

Napoleon Hill
Organiser of the world's first
philosophy of personal achievement.
Author of *'Think And Grow Rich'*,
one of the best selling books of all time.

http://www.naphill.org/

THE KEY TO SUCCESS...

You can read a line and think, 'That's cool'. But will it make you change anything?

The line on the opposite page is a 'cool' sentence. But most people will read it and miss the point.

Napoleon Hill spent over 20 years researching the top achievers in America. His goal was to find their formulae for success.

Remarkably, he found the same one formula applied to them all. The quote opposite can be condensed into the key words - Conceive, believe and achieve.

Most people, if pushed, can conceive a goal – that is, what they want. Most people can take action – the achieve part. But most people have a problem with the 'Believe' part. They don't really believe it's possible.

When you understand how your mind works, you realise how to affect the believe part. But it's one thing to 'intellectually' understand something, and another to 'actually' understand it...

*"Formulate and stamp
indelibly on your mind
a mental picture of yourself
as succeeding.
Hold this picture tenaciously
and never permit it to fade.
Your mind will seek to
develop this picture!"*

Dr. Norman Vincent Peale
1898-1993
Author of
'The Power of Positive Thinking'

How 'Super Achievers' Think

Some people are very good at getting what they want. Let's call them the 'Super Achievers'.

And I'm talking about people who seem to defy logic. People who have literally achieved what was once considered impossible.

It has been shown scientifically, that these people all use their minds in a certain way.

Some of these traits include:
1. They have a clear picture of what they want to achieve. And this picture REALLY excites them.
2. When they think about their goal, they see it as already done.
3. They are totally 1 directional about what they want. That is, they only focus on what they want, never on what they don't.
4. They have a high capacity for giving 100% attention.

Study the lives of people you admire. They will leave clues to their success and these clues will save you time and money. And by the way, the above four points are very, very important!

"Sow a thought and
you reap an act;
Sow an act and you
reap a habit;
Sow a habit and you
reap a character;
Sow a character
and you reap a destiny."

Samuel Smiles
Scottish author and reformer

THE TOOLS OF YOUR MIND ARE THOUGHTS

Thoughts are the building blocks of your life. Realise that a thought is a real thing. If you ever doubt that, just wiggle your thumb! Your dreams start with a thought. The same goes for a nightmare. But you have control over which gets your attention.

See yourself as the movie director of your own life. You can decide now what kind of movie you're going to play in your mind. Will it be sad, or even a horror? Or will it be an exciting adventure full of rewards, happiness and love?

Your thoughts are real and as that wise guy Buddha said, 'Thoughts create your reality'. If you think happy things, you feel happy feelings. It's as simple as that. What you play in the movie house of your mind, gives a result in your life.

Repeated actions lead to habits – good or bad. Your habits result in the quality of your life. Happy habits lead to happiness. Million Dollar habits lead to wealth. Choose your thoughts carefully.

"The greatest discovery of my generation is that human beings can alter their lives by altering their attitudes of mind."

"It is our attitude at the beginning of a difficult task which, more than anything else, will affect its successful outcome."

William James
1842-1910
Psychologist, Philosopher and Author

THIS DETERMINES YOUR LIFE

Two people with the same potential will get different results on a task depending on their attitude.

The right attitude can spark the flame of potential. Similarly, the wrong one can quench it forever.

Your attitude towards everything you do will determine if you achieve it or not. So, learn to pay attention to how your mind is reacting to things in your life.

Realise that your attitude can be influenced by past experiences, conditioning or something someone said. In other words, the voice in your head plays a critical role in 'telling' you how you feel about something or someone!

There is nothing you cannot do with the right attitude. Challenge yourself in your thinking.

Highly successful people always see the outcome as done. To them it's already a done deal. That's what motivates them to keep going.

"A mind too active

is no mind at all."

Theodore Roethke

Pulitzer prize winner for poetry.

Practice The Art Of Mental Relaxation

Your mind works best when it's clear.

It's clear when it's relaxed, and when you're mind is relaxed, your awareness increases dramatically. This means you become more intelligent and get insights about your life. A busy mind very often never sees the opportunities in front of it.

A clear and relaxed mind will be one of the most valuable resources for you as a person. When your mind is relaxed, then you're relaxed. You feel happier, more alive and more connected to life. You're also more creative and in tune with your inner guidance system.

Make a habit of practising mental, not just physical, relaxation. The simplest way I know to do this is to spend time in nature and really be there.

Make a point of doing things you really enjoy as well. Sounds silly, but this is one of the easiest way to relax – namely to lose yourself in doing things you love.

Remember, a happy mind is a relaxed one.

"I will not let anyone walk through my mind with their dirty feet."

Mohandas K. Gandhi
1869-1948
He removed the British from India
without firing a gun.

PROTECT YOUR 'NIGHT CLUB'

When it comes to your mind, you need to be like the biggest and best bouncer at the door of your own nightclub.

This club is the coolest spot in town and you only allow the 'right' people in. You have to be selective in terms of who's refused and who gets access.

People love to make their opinions known and in some cases they may not be in your favour. But it doesn't mean you have to accept their opinion. It's your choice whether you dwell on thoughts that 'bring you down'.

Whether you let them into the nightclub of your mind, and boogie all over the dance floor or not, the choice and responsibility is yours.

Many people are afraid of mind control, yet they have no control over their own mind, let alone their mouths.

Only dwell on the things you like and let the 'right' thoughts into your mind. Your nightclub will be much more successful for it!

You Can If You Think You Can
by Walter D. Wintles

If you think you are beaten, you are;
If you think you dare not, you won't,
If you like to win, but don't think you can, I
t's almost a cinch you won't

If you think you'll lose, you're lost;
For out in the world you find,
Success begins with a fellow's will;
It's all in a state of mind.

For many a game is lost Ere even a play is run,
And many a coward fails
Ere even his work is begun.

Think big and your deed will grow,
Think small and you'll fall behind;
Think that you can and you will,
It's all a state of mind.

If you think you are out-classed, you are;
You've got to think high to rise;
You've got to be sure of yourself before,
You can ever win a prize.

Life battles don't always go
to the stronger or faster man,
But sooner or later, the man who wins
Is the fellow who thinks he can.

YOUR STATE OF MIND

The poem on the right says it all. Read it. Learn it. Live by it. Just remember – a positive state of mind results primarily from a positive mindset, which is more that just 'positive thinking'.

It results from being aware of where your attention is. Of cultivating the habit of thinking more about the things you want to happen than the things you don't.

Are you focusing on the outcomes you really want? Or are you allowing your mind to dwell on things you don't want to happen?

Your unconscious mind is hugely influenced by what you dwell on. It then starts to move you towards what you spend most of your time thinking about.

Think of it like the most advanced missile technology. The cross hairs of the target mechanism are controlled by how you think.

What target are you focusing on? Is it the thing you want to happen or the thing you don't?

"If you use your mind to study reality, you won't understand either your mind or reality. If you study reality without using your mind, you'll understand both. People capable of true vision, know that the mind is empty."

Bodhidharma
A legendary Buddhist monk

GET OUT OF THE WAY OF THE POWER.

This one might confuse you.

But it's probably the most important and most difficult for your mind to grasp. Your mind is a wonderful tool, but it's not you. The real you. The real you is the spirit behind your mind. The spirit that is connected to all life.

There is a universal life force. This force or energy flows through everything living. Plants, trees, animals and yes, us. Human beings. You and me. It connects us all.

Our minds/egos love to be in control. But this higher life force is always there to guide us in right action and is outside your mind's control.

When your mind is relaxed and clear, you allow a space for this life force to come through.

Your mind is a tool for enjoying life. Your life energy is mission control. It knows the next step. Always.

There are those who know how to step outside their mind. Find them and learn from them.

CHAPTER 3

ADVICE FROM GREATS

Advice from a great writer   47

Advice from a great spiritual giant   49

Advice from a great leader   51

Advice from a great movie maker   53

Advice from a great thinker   55

Advice from a great mountaineer   57

Advice from a great hero   59

Advice from a great Saint   61

Advice from a great woman   63

Advice from a great artist   65

"Keep away from small people who try to belittle your ambitions. Small people always do that, but the really great make you feel that you, too, can become great."

Mark Twain

1835-1910

Writer, Humorist AND Lecturer

ADVICE FROM A GREAT WRITER

Be careful who you surround yourself with, for they will influence who you become.

People usually fall into one of two categories – Dream Makers or Dream Breakers.

Which one do you want to be around?

The Dream Makers will see the potential in you and the world around you. They ask why not as opposed to why? - Which is what the Dream Breakers ask.

Anyone who is truly successful will always encourage others to achieve the same success. Seek these people out and remember to be one yourself.

Your words carry as much weight as anyone else's. Choose them well. The right words can live on forever. The man on the far page is a case in point.

"Believe nothing merely because you have been told it. Do not believe what your teacher tells you merely out of respect for the teacher. Believe nothing, no matter where you read it, or who said it, no matter if I have said it, unless it agrees with your own reason and your own common sense."

Buddha

Otherwise known as Siddhartha Gautama.

The enlightened one.

ADVICE FROM
A GREAT
SPIRITUAL GIANT

Everything must be measured by results. Listen to all with an open mind but test their advice to see if it works for you.

Be courageous enough to challenge someone's viewpoint if it does not make sense. But be different from the cynic.

A cynic is someone whose mind is so closed they will try nothing new. They are looking to prove you wrong before you open your mouth.

They will shoot down an idea or opinion before giving it a chance or testing to see if it has any merit.

Being open implies listening fully and then being willing to try something new, without looking through the expectation of it not working.

The point here is to have an open mind and yet, always measure the results.

"Even as a student,
I saw many young men
who had great natural ability,
but who did not have the
self-discipline and patience
to build on their endowment."

Nelson Mandela.

First President of South Africa to be elected in
fully-representative democratic elections.

ADVICE FROM A GREAT LEADER

Talent is quite common. What's uncommon, unfortunately, is making full use of that talent.

Very often the person who excels is the one with average talent combined with extraordinary drive and ambition. The one with passion.

One of the secrets to getting this drive is to have a clear vision of where you want to go in all areas of your life. And critically, that vision has to excite every part of your being. You have to really, really, really, really want it!

Being given the gift of a talent is worthless unless you develop the art of persistence and discipline to harness your full potential.

Many people like to talk about all the things they will do. But few ever do them. Success lies in the doing. A super achiever, like Nelson Mandela, is someone who has decided what they want and then persist, no matter what, until they get it.

*"You have to find something
that you love enough to
be able to take risks, jump
over the hurdles and break
through the brick walls that
are always going to be
placed in front of you.
If you don't have that kind
of feeling for what it is you
are doing, you'll stop
at the first giant hurdle."*

George Lucas

Film Director and Producer
He made a small movie called Star Wars...

ADVICE FROM A GREAT MOVIE MAKER

Mr. Lucas gives a hint here of what differentiates the mindset of a great achiever from the average person.

If you get nothing else from this book other than understanding this point it will change your life and the people around you forever. To find what you love to do and may take some contemplation and experimentation. But it's time well spent. Some answers may be found in answering the following questions:

- If you knew you couldn't fail, what would you love to do?

- If you won the lottery today, what are the things you'd love to do?

- If you only had 12 months to live, what are the things you'd do?

Be aware that very few people ever ask these questions of every area of their life. Even George Lucas probably hasn't. Why not have it all? Great health, great relationships, great career and lots of fun. When you identify what you love, you ignite you fuel cells of passion. And then anything is possible. Anything.

"I count him braver who overcomes his desires than him who conquers his enemies, for the hardest victory is over self."

Aristotle

Smart Greek guy and student of Plato

ADVICE FROM A GREAT THINKER

'Victory over self' sounds simple but in practice it can be challenging. But the challenge is well worth the rewards.

Science is now proving what philosophers and great thinkers have been saying for millennia. That we literally are what we think, and that we are largely controlled, at the moment, by our unconscious minds.

Our unconscious plays a vital role in every part of our lives. It regulates the amazing vehicle that is our body and it 'tells' us what to expect in every area of our lives – from relationships to health, success to fun.

'Victory over self' means being in control of what you think. Being in control of your own mind. Rather than drifting along according to the expectations of your mind.

Be aware that this IS possible and that areas of your life where you may have settled for 2nd best can be re-energised by the way you think. (Read chapter 2 on the mind for more clues!)

"You don't have to be a fantastic hero to do certain things; to compete. You can be just an ordinary person, sufficiently motivated to reach challenging goals. The intense effort, the giving of everything you've got, is a very pleasant bonus."

"It is not the mountain we conquer but ourselves."

Sir Edmund Hillary
New Zealand Mountaineer.
He and Tenzin Norgay were the
first men to climb Mount Everest.

Advice From A Great Mountaineer

Avoid falling into the trap of thinking 'That could never happen to me' for it would be a tragedy.

People who achieve outstanding results in any field at one point hadn't. Maybe all they had was a dream or an idea.

Climbing a mountain, is a simple analogy for climbing the heights in pursuit of your goals and desires. You can only do it one step at a time and it takes preparation, practice, determination and staying focused on the ultimate goal – reaching the top.

Along the way you may have to overcome or ignore distractions and obstacles, many of them mental. But persistence pays off.

And be aware that one of the pleasant side effects is the feeling of intense pleasure and satisfaction in moving towards and then achieving a challenging goal.

Just start. You can do it.

"A hero is an ordinary individual who finds the strength to persevere and endure in spite of overwhelming obstacles."

Christopher Reeve

1952-2004

Actor, Director, Producer, Writer and Speaker.

Famous for being 'SuperMan'

ADVICE FROM A GREAT HERO

One of life's great ironies. The man who played Superman in the original movie, ended up in a wheel chair.

But Christopher Reeves inspired more people from that position than many people who have the gift of movement ever did.

Are you a hero in waiting?

This could be the time for you to go after that something you've been dreaming of, but putting on the long finger.

Start from where you're at right now and do what you can, no matter how lofty your dream seems to be.

You will have setbacks sure, but it's your call whether you want to be your own hero. It'd be nice to look in the mirror one day and think, 'You inspire me.'

"Start by doing what's necessary, then what's possible, and suddenly you are doing the impossible."

St. Francis of Assisi
1181-1226
Founder of the Franciscan Order
and patron saint of animals, merchants,
Italy and the environment.

ADVICE FROM
A GREAT SAINT

The mechanics of how to live a great life have been around for thousands of years. It's just that people don't always listen and more importantly, they've been conditioned to not believe.

So let's say you know what you want, but maybe you aren't sure where to start. St. Francis gives us a clue.

Once you're clear on what you want, start from where you are. Take whatever steps you can see right now and then the next steps to take will reveal themselves.

Keep focused on your dream and keep moving. One day you will wake up and your life will be what you once considered impossible.

As the saying goes, impossible is not a fact, it's only an opinion.

"The more you praise and celebrate your life, the more there is in life to celebrate."

Oprah Winfrey
TV Personality, Producer and Author.
Richest African-American of the 21st century.

ADVICE FROM
A GREAT WOMAN

One of the most successful business women ever,
when Oprah gives advice women and men all over
the world listen and as well as being financially
successful beyond her wildest dreams, it's fantastic
to know that she has made a vital and positive
difference to people's lives all around the world. You
could have worse role models.

Her words contain an important lesson. Even
though you may not be where you really want to
be right now, there are always things in your life to
appreciate and enjoy. Once you start to look for
these things, you'll find you'll notice more and more
of them.

Take the time to celebrate them, to savour them.
Strangely, the more you do this, the more things
you'll find coming into your life to celebrate.

What value is there in achieving your dreams
but being miserable? The secret to happiness
and fulfilment is enjoying what you have now. To
cultivate the habit of really appreciating life.

*"The greater danger
for most of us is not that
our aim is too high
and we miss it,
but that it is too low
and we reach it."*

Michelangelo Buonarroti

1474-1564

Italian Renaissance Painter and Sculptor

ADVICE FROM
A GREAT ARTIST

How big do you think? Are you afraid of thinking big? Of dreaming only to end up disappointed? Most people set small goals. That is, goals that they know they will definitely achieve.

You are a being of limitless potential. Science has now proven this. You are capable of living the life of your dreams.

Michelangelo reminds us that the worst thing that can happen from aiming high is that we still end up higher than where we started.

Too many people set uninspiring goals. And so they live uninspiring and dull lives.

If you want to live a life of fulfilment, why not follow the advice of one of the most creative minds to ever walk this planet?

Think as BIG as you can and go for it!

CHAPTER 4

MAKING FRIENDS EFFORTLESSLY

Listen   69

See everyone as your equal   71

Use this curve   73

Use their name   75

Really appreciate people   77

When you're wrong admit it.   79

Say this when it's true   81

Your attitude affects your relationships   83

Be yourself…no matter what   85

"*You can make more friends in two months by becoming interested in other people than you can in two years by trying to get other people interested in you.*"

Dale Carnegie

1888-1955

Author and Trainer

Author of

'*How to win friends and influence people*'.

This book is well worth a read.

THE QUICKEST WAY TO MAKE FRIENDS

Many people find it difficult to make friends. It's really quite simple. But simple things aren't always easy to do. One of the master secrets to making friends is to be genuinely interested in other people. Find out about their lives. Find out about their hopes and dreams. Take an interest in another and you will have a friend for life.

Above all, when you're with them, give 100% attention. The best communicators make you feel like you're the only person in the room. In fact, even if all you do is listen to the other person, you'll find that they considered it a 'wonderful conversation'.

Most people are too busy with their lives and too busy in their heads to be genuinely interested in you. If you can learn to shut off the 'chatter' in your mind and switch off your 'what can I get out of this person?' button, then you'll be 1 in a thousand.

Plus, as well as making lots of new friends by genuinely giving people 100% attention, you'll also get the benefit of learning new things!

"You have 1 mouth

and 2 ears.

Use them in that ratio."

Anonymous

LISTEN

The average listener nods their head while the other person is talking, pretending to be listening, yet all the while, they are just waiting for the chance to say what they want to say.

The good listener pays attention. Really. People know instinctively when you're genuinely listening. They pick up on it unconsciously. Probably because it's so rare. And true listening is very rare. It takes practice and commitment.

Most conversations are really a reaction to what's been said before. You say something and I think of something that happened to me, or another story and I wait for a chance to tell you, all the while missing what you're saying to me. All the while, not hearing 'you'.

If you can cultivate the true art of listening, you will have a skill that attracts people to you like no other. You'll be fighting them away. People crave attention. They crave the respect of other human beings. And by getting it from you, they never forget you. Ever.

"After the game,

the king and pawn

go into the same box."

Italian Proverb

SEE EVERYONE AS YOUR EQUAL

Everyone on the planet has the same rights as you. Regardless of colour, race, beliefs, religion, wealth or lack of, we are all human beings.

Never see yourself as being above someone else. And never see yourself lesser than another. Some may not use their potential, that is their choice. And others may use it to serve different ends than you.

Respect everyone and be open to learning from everyone.

Every person has their own talent. Every person is a unique expression of life. Avoid falling into the trap of looking down on someone or alternatively, putting someone up on a pedestal.

Everyone deserves your respect. You are no lesser nor greater than any other human being.

"The curve that can set

a lot of things straight

is a smile."

Anonymous

USE THIS CURVE

People are automatically attracted to someone who is smiling (maybe because it's so rare!). In fact, it can be very like yawning – contagious in crowds! This is a great way of warming people to you. Even if you fake it, you feel better! Try it.

If you can train yourself to smile when you meet people, you'll be amazed at how positively they react to you.

Realise that most people are waiting to see if you like them. A genuine, bright, heart-warming smile says 'I like you'. And in return, people automatically return the sentiment.

Dogs and babies live by the same principle. There are no conditions attached. Think of a dog wagging it's tail in delight at seeing you or the baby giggling with happiness when it sees you. Bottom line is they like you first and so you react positively to them (or you should!)

So maybe you can take the lead from now on and be the one who smiles first. Who knows, maybe you'll end up changing the world?

*"Remember that a
person's name is to
that person the sweetest
and most important sound
in any language."*

From
'How to win friends and influence people'
by Dale Carnegie

USE THEIR NAME

This is a sort of trick, but it's harmless and people with very strong social skills use it all the time.

When you're talking to someone, use the person's name throughout your conversation.

When you use a person's name, it's like telling them you really like them. It seems to hit an unconscious trigger that automatically opens them up to you.

As Dale Carnegie also said, "If you want to win friends, make it a point to remember them. If you remember my name, you pay me a subtle compliment; you indicate that I have made an impression on you. Remember my name and you add to my feeling of importance."

But just be sure not to do it too much – over use can create an impression of being false, so moderation is advised!

"The deepest principle in human nature is the craving to be appreciated."

William James

A very smart American

REALLY APPRECIATE PEOPLE

This is so simple, it's often ignored. Many people take others for granted. If you meet someone who has many genuine friends you will find that they always have one trait common to them. They genuinely appreciate the people they know.

This doesn't mean showering people with expensive gifts or trying to 'buy' friendship. All it means is really valuing people for who they are and expressing that in whatever way you feel is appropriate. When you do this, genuinely, it comes across in everything you say and do.

And people gravitate to it.

Appreciation always gets you further than criticism. Always. Business managers, teachers and coaches in all fields, could learn a lot from that statement.

"Swallow your pride

occasionally,

it's not fattening."

Frank Tyger

A guy with a lot of smart quotes.

WHEN YOU'RE WRONG, ADMIT IT.

If you can say 'I'm wrong' and say it with meaning, you will be one of an elite few that command respect in the eyes of the many.

For some reason, the human ego finds it very difficult to admit when it's made a mistake. Yet, we all make mistakes every day. In fact, the great achievers of our time say that unless we're making mistakes, we can't be making progress.

The ability to admit you're wrong is second only to the ability of saying the words mentioned when you turn the page...

"Saying 'I'm sorry',
and really meaning it,
is the best relationship
builder in the world.
And best of all,
it only takes two seconds"

Shane Cradock

Say This When It's True...

'I'm sorry.'

It takes two seconds to say these words, but sometimes they never come out. Very often in life, everyone else is to blame and even when we've done something that we know is wrong, we can find clever ways to justify our lack of apology.

Being the first to say 'sorry', genuinely, even when you have been wronged by others, can very often trigger a positive reaction when you least expect it.

The worst case is when all parties are right, no-one is wrong but now, we don't have a relationship or friendship anymore.

The most important question to ask yourself is 'what's important here?' Being right all the time, or the relationship you have with someone?

Can you see the difference?

"Our life is what our thoughts make it. A man will find that as he alters his thoughts toward things and other people, things and other people will alter towards him."

James Allen
1864-1912,
Author of "As A Man Thinketh"

YOUR ATTITUDE AFFECTS YOUR RELATIONSHIPS.

Many people find fault with others. "They didn't do this or they didn't do that." "Aren't they terrible? If only they could be more like me.. Basically, it's all their fault! Not yours!

How you look at things and think about things, directly affects how you behave. This is especially true when it comes to people.

If you think someone is annoying or troublesome, then everything they do will be seen through this 'filter'. If you look through a dirty window, everything seems dirty!

So, be aware that how you see people, affects how they are with you. And very often when you clean the dirty window, the person miraculously changes too!

But let's be realistic. Sometimes the person could just be a nasty piece of work. And in that case, it can be best to just walk away.

There are plenty of others out there open to a bit of your sunshine!

"This above all:

To thine own self be true.

And it must follow as

the night the day,

thou canst not then be false

to any man."

William Shakespeare

A great English writer.
Probably the greatest.

BE YOURSELF...
NO MATTER WHAT

Everyone has their own unique impression to leave in the world. Their own talents to be expressed. Do the things you love to do and take pride in them, provided of course they are grounded in principles of love, integrity and respect.

Being yourself in a world that often encourages conformity and uniformity can be challenging. Standing up for what you believe in, in the face of opposition, can be one of the most challenging things you can ever do. Yet such moments, are what the world changes on.

More than ever, the world needs people to be truly who they are. To express themselves in a way that respects people and the planet. To create their own unique path in life.

And be aware, that when you show people you are prepared to be yourself, some around you may not like it. But there are plenty of people out there who will love the real you.

CHAPTER 5

THE ART OF COMMUNICATION

The value of communication   91

Speak when you have something to say   93

When you say nothing at all   95

The Holy Grail of communication   97

A skill to be learned   99

Say it in plain English   101

The gift of all great communicators   103

When people disagree   105

Work at it   107

Without this, there is no communication 109

"The basic building block of
good communications
is the feeling that every
human being is
unique and of value."

Unknown author

THE VALUE OF COMMUNICATION

The ability to communicate clearly with others is a skill that should be taught in every school across the world. The ability to get across your point of view, to sell your ideas, and to learn the meaning of genuine listening are priceless skills.

To neglect your communication ability is to neglect your right to a great life. People who achieve their dreams are those who generally are great communicators. Leaders, visionaries and achievers have all mastered this important skill.

The umbrella of communication covers many areas like selling, public speaking, listening, writing, performing, relationships, managing people and so on. It's a vital life skill.

There are many ways to improve your skills but you need to recognise the importance of why you need to. Once you do, a fundamental value in becoming a great communicator is well articulated in the quote opposite. When you really respect people, you will funnily enough always command respect in your actions and words.

"Wise men talk because they have something to say; fools, because they have to say something."

Plato

Ancient Greek philosopher.
Student of Socrates.

SPEAK WHEN YOU HAVE SOMETHING TO SAY

Ever heard the expression 'He loved the sound of his own voice'?

Many people really do. So much so, that they will talk just for the sake of having others 'apparently' listen to them.
The tragedy is that those who have little to offer the world often speak endlessly, while those who really have something to day stay quiet. So many words are wasted every day around the world, by people speaking just for the sake of exercising their vocal chords.

So there are two points here. The first is to respect silence. You don't have to speak but if you decide to, at least ensure it's interesting for your audience!

And secondly, just because someone speaks all the time, doesn't mean that they're actually saying anything. They could be that fool Plato is referring to!

"Saying nothing...

sometimes says the most."

Emily Dickinson

Famous American poet

WHEN YOU SAY NOTHING AT ALL...

What can I say?

"You cannot truly listen to anyone and do anything else at the same time."

M. Scott Peck

American psychiatrist and author of
'The Road Less Travelled.'

THE HOLY GRAIL OF COMMUNICATION

What is it? It's a learned skill that explains why, after meeting with a master communicator, you feel like the only person in the room.

People know instinctively when you're doing it and as soon as you're not, they pick up on it unconsciously.

What am I speaking about?

The ability to really pay attention, to really listen. Not just to the words being spoken but to the emotion, the silence between the words, the tone and to listen with your heart and eyes.

To listen to someone, means to pay 100% attention to that person. It doesn't mean nodding your head respectfully, all the while waiting for a slight pause so that you can get your point in.

Master the art of genuine listening and you will have friends wherever you go in the world.

"The ability to speak eloquently is not to be confused with having something to say."

Michael P. Hart

A SKILL THAT MUST BE LEARNED...

When asked of their biggest fears in life, people all over the world consistently name one fear as being their biggest.

Public speaking. The act of standing in front of a group of people and expressing your point of view. The irony is that if you can put your point of view across clearly to one person, then you can do it to a thousand. It's just a few more ears...

All great speakers started somewhere and you can be sure that they made plenty of mistakes. And even if you don't desire to wow audiences across the world with your verbal prowess, the ability to stand in front of others and communicate your point of view is something that all people would love to be able to do.

Funnily enough, it won't happen sitting in front of the TV. It takes desire, practice, practice and even more practice. Anyone can become proficient at public speaking. To start pick up a book, buy a CD or join a group. Or even start talking to yourself in the mirror. Oh, and by the way, even if you are good at public speaking, you can always get better...so keep practicing!

"Elegance of language may not be in the power of all of us; but simplicity and straight forwardness are. Write much as you would speak; speak as you think. If with your inferior, speak no coarser than usual; if with your superiors, no finer. Be what you say; and, within the rules of prudence, say what you are."

Henry Alford

English scholar and writer

IN PLAIN ENGLISH...

It's amazing how many people get stuck when it comes to writing a letter or tongue tied if they find themselves having to say a few words in front of a TV camera. It's as if they believe they're expected to transform into some 'super guru' person they have in their mind, and not be themselves.

The simplest way to write something is in using the words you'd use if you were explaining it to someone in front of you. This is natural and easy.

The simplest way to say something in front of a TV camera is as if the camera wasn't there. That's what's meant by being a 'natural'. It's just the ability to be yourself, regardless of the situation.

And remember, communication is mostly about tone and body language. Words are a tiny percentage of communication.

When trying to say the important things, just say them from the heart. Sincerity shines through all words.

"If there is any great secret

of success in life,

it lies in the ability

to put yourself in the

other person's place

and to see things

from his point of view –

as well as your own."

Henry Ford

The man with the cars.

THE GIFT OF ALL GREAT COMMUNICATORS...

When you put yourself in the shoes of another and look at the world through their eyes, you get tremendous insight into what motivates them, what scares them and what makes the difference with them.

Of course, most people are too preoccupied with their own world to take interest in how another sees the world. 'My way or the highway' is usually their slogan.

Even the great philosophers saw the value in looking through another's eyes. One game they would often play, is debating one point of view and then switching sides, and debating the other point of view just as passionately.

They believed that what would be left, would be the truth. And if nothing else, the process would broaden their minds.

Cultivating the ability to look through another's eyes, as well as looking through your own will allow you to make more informed decisions and to speak in the other's interests.

Your world needs a bit more of this.

"If you say what you think

don't expect to hear

only what you like."

Malcolm Forbes

Publisher of Forbes magazine

KEEPING YOUR FRIENDS

I know quite a few people who get upset if people disagree with their point of view. And these are very plain speaking, forthright individuals.

This quote reminds us to expect different points of view. In fact, it's a good thing.

The people who are respected the most in life are those who say what they think and believe, regardless of others' opinions.

So if you want a world where you're allowed and free to say what you think and feel, doesn't it make sense that others should be given the same courtesy?

A world where people speak their truth is a good thing, once we have a culture of openness and respect for differing views.

Being direct and honest is great. Just expect it back and be cool with it.

*"The difference between
the right word and the
almost right word is
the difference between
lightning and a lightning bug."*

Mark Twain

WORK AT IT

Effortless communication takes commitment, time and practice. It takes putting yourself in challenging situations and being tested. It requires openness to making mistakes, and learning from them.

Every word you speak, and the way you say it can have a massive impact on your audience. But it takes a committed communicator to know exactly how to make that impact.
The ability to tell a story and have people on the edge of their seats or to present to a board-room full of people and have them intrigued by your every word, all takes practice.
And yes, anyone can become great. Anyone can learn the necessary skills. It just takes commitment, time and practice.

The truly great communicators all have one particular skill in common. It's one of the reasons they are so easy to listen to. In fact, it makes them all the more intriguing.

What is it? The gift of saying a lot, in as few words as possible.

"The problem with communication is the illusion that is has occurred."

George Bernard Shaw

Irish playwright and winner of
the Nobel prize for literature.

WITHOUT THIS, THERE IS NO COMMUNICATION

You can stand in front of people, and make a speech but how do you know you're communicating? How do you know you're getting your message across?

How often do you say something but it's heard differently to what you meant? Has anyone ever done something even though you asked them not to?

This is the mystery of communication. And as the sender of the message you have to take responsibility.   Particularly as you now realise that most people are very poor listeners.
Always get feedback from your audience. Find out what they took from your communication. This will tell you whether your intentions were achieved.

Be open to getting feedback on all aspects of your communication – written, spoken, and visual. This is the best way to improve.

CHAPTER 6

ACHIEVING
YOUR DREAMS

The first step   113

What is success to you?   115

Move towards your dreams   117

Keep taking action   119

Do your absolute best right now   121

Have a goal and a plan   123

Never accept 'impossible'   125

This is key....Act as if...   127

Practice, practice, practice   129

Be unrelenting   131

*"The first step to a great life
is to fill your life with a
positive faith that will
help you through anything.
The second is to
begin where you are."*

Dr. Norman Vincent Peale

THE FIRST STEP...

Self-trust and faith are linked to each other. When you trust your abilities and yourself, faith kicks in. You know that anything can happen and you will deal with it. You believe in yourself.

Once you have that, it doesn't matter where you start from. It doesn't matter what's before you. The book stores are filled with stories of men and women who have overcome adversity and horrific situations to lead fulfilling and successful lives.

The danger is that we can look at someone else's life and say 'I want that now!' Fine, but you must start from where you are. You have your own path to follow, your own story, your own dream.

We can shut ourselves down before we get going, because the mountain of our dreams can look too high. But you achieve one step at a time. That means starting where you are.

*"To laugh often and love much;
to win the respect of intelligent
persons and the affection of
children; to earn the approbation
of honest citizens and endure
the betrayal of false friends; to
appreciate beauty; to find the best
in others; to give of one's self; to
leave the world a bit better, whether
by a healthy child, a garden patch
or a redeemed social condition;
to have played and laughed
with enthusiasm and sung with
exultation; to know even one life has
breathed easier because you have
lived – this is to have succeeded."*

Ralph Waldo Emerson

WHAT IS SUCCESS
TO YOU?

Success can mean different things to different people.

Society may tell you that to be seen as successful, you must have a lot of money, a big car, a big house and look and dress like a model. But realise that many people who have the above aren't necessarily happy.

The point here is that you and only you can determine what success means to you. It may be to live life as you wish, to have great health, to be happy and have great friends or to have it all!

More and more people are waking up to the fact that they can determine how their lives are. And they're realising having only material success can be hollow.

True success is very much related to making a beneficial difference to people and the world.

Wisdom literature through the ages has revealed one common value to people who live successful and fulfilling lives. A clue to this value is within the quote.

*"I have learned this at
least by my experiment:
that if one advances
confidently in the direction
of his dreams, and
endeavours to live the life
he has imagined, he will meet
with a success unexpected
in common hours."*

Henry David Thoreau
1817-1862
Writer and Poet

MOVE TOWARDS YOUR DREAMS

When you've decided exactly how you wish your life to be, and taken the time to clarify it, you must take this next step, where so many others stop.

You have to believe that you will achieve the life you wish and keep taking steps towards it. When you keep persisting, you will find that things will start falling into place.

Of course, it may take some time. When you're boiling water, it takes a lot of heat before you see anything happening. You could be fooled into thinking that nothing is happening at all and then the next minute, there's steam.

Achieving you're goals, dreams and ideal life can be a lot like that. So you must keep moving into your life with an expectancy that the things you want are going to happen.

Critical to all of this is the power of your imagination. Spend time imagining yourself in your ideal life. This sends a strong signal to your unconscious mind about the direction you're going. Remember, you move towards what you focus on.

"Achievement seems to be connected with action. Successful men and women keep moving. They make mistakes, but they don't quit."

Conrad Hilton

1887-1979
Founder of Hilton Hotels

Keep Taking Action

Nelson Mandela once said that 'Vision without action is merely daydreaming. Action without vision is only passing the time. But vision with action can change the world.'

The above quote really says it all about how action can work wonders, in the context of having a dream.

Realise that so few people have any vision of their future bar the next pay check. Sure they may dream of better things, but all too often fear can stop them from taking any action at all.

And when there is no action, there will be no change. Once you have your vision, keep taking action and you will change your world and the world around you.

Just include us all in your picture. It'd be nice to think that by you achieving all of the things you wish for, we all benefit in the process.

"My philosophy is that not only are you responsible for your life, but doing the best at this moment puts you in the best place for the next moment."

"There is no discrimination against excellence."

Oprah Winfrey

Do Your Absolute Best Right Now...

The people who get on in the world are the people who play with the cards they're dealt.

They don't moan about the situation they're in, they just get on with it. Oprah Winfrey is a person who has overcome very tough situations in her life to achieve a phenomenal lifestyle. Her simple philosophy is one adopted by many successful people. Deal with what's in front of you right now to the very best of your ability.

By doing this, it does something very simple. Your attitude changes to a very positive one. And this alone, will rub off into your life.

When your attitude changes, your life starts to look brighter. You also start to enjoy yourself more, because when you do your best at anything, you have to be fully involved – and that is one of the secrets to happiness.

Her second quote is pure magic. Oprah undoubtedly encountered much prejudice and discrimination over her lifetime. But her answer was always to do her best. To be excellent at what she did. That solved everything.

"I find it fascinating that most people plan their vacations with better care than they plan their lives. Perhaps that is because escape is easier than change."

Jim Rohn

Author and Speaker

HAVE A GOAL
AND A PLAN…

You don't need a goal or a plan to be happy.

Being happy is a state of mind. But if you want to change your life and achieve your dreams and things you'd like, then it's essential to have a clear picture of your goal.

A friend of mind once said, 'The only way to eat an elephant is one piece at a time'. This is where a plan comes in. It helps you break something down into more manageable steps. It might seem like a very BIG goal, but any big goal is just a series of small goals put together.

The quotes on the opposite page are common sense but sense isn't always that common.

A very small percentage of the population write down their goals in life. Most people spend more time planning their holidays than they do their lives. Which is a tragedy, because a small amount of goal setting and planning in your life can change it forever.

"All things are possible until they are proved impossible - and even the impossible may only be so, as of now."

Pearl S. Buck
1892-1973
Novelist

NEVER ACCEPT THE IMPOSSIBLE.

The history of the world is the impossible becoming possible.

Almost everything you take for granted in your life, at one time was an impossibility. Can you imagine time travelling back to the year 1900 and explaining some of the following to people?

A cell phone
A television
A car
A plane
The internet
Man landing on the moon and exploring the universe.

We live in an age of possibility. All of the above would seem miraculous to someone living in 1900. But that's only just over 100 years ago. Look around you now. You will see things that at one point were just an idea in someone's mind. Your watch. A chair. Your computer.

So, is there anything you'd like to do be or have that just seems impossible? Maybe you should rethink it.

*"Act like the person
you want to become.
For as Goethe, the German
philosopher, once wrote,
'Before you can do
something, you first
must be something.'"*

Napoleon Hill

THIS IS KEY...
ACT AS IF...

This point can easily be lost. And it's so important.

If you wish to achieve something in your life that you don't have right now, picture yourself having achieved it and ask yourself this question.

What kind of person am I?

Really look into this. How do I feel? Am I relaxed, confident, happy? How do I look? How do I sound? What's going through my mind? How do I look at life?

Really figure out how the future you is. Then once you're clear on this, start acting like that person. If this is the future you, you desire, then why bother waiting. Start behaving like the way you're going to be.

This has an amazingly powerful affect on your unconscious mind. You are literally re-programming your onboard computer.

And it works. Try it. But try it consistently.

"If people only knew how hard I work to gain my mastery, it wouldn't seem so wonderful at all."

Michelangelo Buonarroti
1475-1564
Artist

PRACTICE, PRACTICE, PRACTICE

In an age of instant gratification, people can expect to get everything they want instantly.

They read stories about people who have become 'overnight' sensations. While some people have made massive jumps overnight, what isn't always spoken about are the years they've been practising their art, career or chosen profession. Success requires dedication and as the saying goes 'The only place success comes before work is in the dictionary.'

Whatever you wish to succeed at will require practice. Funnily enough, when you're doing something you love, practice is only a word. You love doing what you do.

Having a clear picture of the benefits to you and the world can also serve as powerful motivation whenever you encounter roadblocks on your journey.

Michelangelo's quote is funny because he is considered to have been one of most successful artists to have ever lived. Yet, he points out that he is only successful because of how much work he put in to gain mastery.

"Desire is the key to motivation, but it's the determination and commitment to an unrelenting pursuit of your goal - a commitment to excellence - that will enable you to attain the success you seek."

Mario Andretti

World Class Race Car Driver

Be Unrelenting...

How much do you want what you're looking for in your life? You have to really, really, really, really want it. It has to ignite all of the cells of passion within your body. That's why it's so important for you to define your own meaning of success.

Once you've decided on your goal, you must be prepared to do whatever it takes to achieve it. The passion will help fuel your commitment, despite any apparent obstacles or setbacks.

Remember, really go for it in every area of your life. Health, Fun, Relationships, Financial, Business, Personal and Contribution.

Be clear on what you want in every area of your life, not just one. Too many have focused on one area only to get there and realise they'd messed up on their health or relationships.

Spend time clarifying what you really want. Seek out your passion.

Is the life of your dreams worth that?

CHAPTER 7

BEING SUCCESSFUL & HAPPY

Be like the turtle   135

Success is what you become   137

Your habits and concentration   139

Commit yourself 100%   141

Overall approach   143

Reality Check   145

How to deal with criticism   147

Dress for success   149

Starting where you are   151

Having balls   153

"Behold the turtle.

He only makes progress

when he sticks his neck out."

James Bryant Conant
1893-1978,
Past President of Harvard University

BE LIKE THE TURTLE...

...And take a few risks.

Too many can be crippled with fear. The fear of failure, of making a mistake, or even the fear of success!

One thing is for certain. If you're going for your dreams, you will have to stick your neck out.

Very often that can mean doing things that no-one else understands. It might mean being criticised.

Realise that the majority of people have dreams, but the herd mentality can keep them from doing anything. And if another member of the herd starts to move away, they can react.

Sticking your neck out implies taking risks. It also implies standing out from the crowd or the herd. It could even mean that you stand up and say something that no-one else agrees with.

You will make mistakes, but you will also learn.

"The highest reward

for a man's toil is

not what he gets for it

but what he becomes by it."

John Ruskin

Author, poet, artist and critic.

SUCCESS IS WHAT YOU BECOME

This is usually not seen as the big benefit of achieving success.

To be successful implies discipline, dedication, persistence, courage, focus and a positive mental attitude. To name but a few traits.

The character you develop as you move towards your vision of a better future, is something that cannot be taken away from you.

You could make a million and lose it all. You could have a magnificent house, only to see it burn to the ground.

But the skills and inner qualities you develop in the pursuit of your goal can never be taken away from you. And these are the things that are of real value.

Another way of putting the quote opposite is, 'Don't become successful for what you get. Become successful for what it makes you become.'

*"I never could have done
what I have done without
the habits of punctuality,
order, and diligence, without
the determination
to concentrate myself
on one subject at a time."*

Charles Dickens
1812-1870
Writer

Your Habits And Concentration

We are creatures of habit. At least 95% of our actions are unconscious every day. This is an amazing statistic.

Of course, we all have good habits and bad habits. If we are to achieve what we desire, we most likely are going to have to create habits that support the achievement of our goals. For example, if we want to get into good shape and maintain it, we may have to adjust our eating and exercise habits.

A habit is installed by repetition. Eventually it becomes automatic so that we don't have to think about it. Just like riding a bicycle.

You can become excellent at anything by developing the right habits. When you've decided on your goals, ask yourself what habits will I need to achieve these?

People who excel have developed successful habits. You can model them. The great writer, Dickens, highlights some of his good habits. He also points out one habit common to all successful people. They have trained themselves to focus 100% on one thing at a time.

"Until one is committed there is hesitancy,
the chance to draw back, always
ineffectiveness. Concerning all acts
of initiative (and creation), there is one
elementary truth, the ignorance of which kills
countless ideas and splendid plans:
That the moment one definitely commits
oneself, then providence moves too.
All sorts of things occur to help one
that would never otherwise have occurred.
A whole stream of events issues from the
decision, raising in one's favour all manner
of unforeseen incidents and meetings and
material assistance, which no man could
have dreamt would have come his way.
I have learned a deep respect
for one of Goethe's couplets:
"Whatever you can do,
or dream you can, begin it.
Boldness has genius, power and magic in it."

W.H. Murray
from The Scottish Himalayan Expedition

COMMIT YOURSELF 100%

Please read and re-read the paragraphs opposite. They contain so much. You can dream up the life you long for. You can set lofty goals and have all of your plans worked out on paper.

But unless, you make a decision in your heart that you're really going to go for it, you could sabotage yourself.

Commitment implies your heart and soul agreeing that this is what is for you. Your will hardens and you will accept nothing less.

When you get to this point, something inexplicable happens. As you start to take action, you will find that things will go your way more than not. The right people will pop up at the right time. Luck will go your way.

It's simple to read this page and think 'Yeah, I understand that'. But this is so subtle, you could live your entire life and not really get it.

Go for it. Whatever you can do, do it. Magic is waiting there to lend a hand.

"Act without doing;
work without effort.
Think of the small as large
and the few as many.
Confront the difficult
while it is still easy;
accomplish the great task
by a small series
of small acts."

From the Tao Te Ching
(Roughly translated as
'The Book Of The Way and Its Virtue')

Overall
Approach

Instead of reading a page of my words, I really
believe it's worth reading the words opposite several
times. Reflect on them.

They are simple words but very, very powerful.

"He who works his land will have abundant food, but he who chases fantasies lacks judgement."

Proverbs 12:11

From the writings of the Old Testament

REALITY CHECK

It's great to have fun dreams and inspiring goals, and to act like you're there already. So, does this mean you walk around with your head in the clouds? Well, some people do but it's not to be encouraged.

People who achieve their goals, have the ability to strike a balance between having a picture of their future and knowing exactly where they are right now. They are in touch with reality.

Start from where you are. If you haven't written a book but you'd like to, start writing. If you want to direct a movie but you dream one day of doing it, then start. Just start.

Work with what you have right now. Your talent, your level of income, your time, your health. Keep an eye on the top of the mountain you're climbing. This quote reminds us to take stock of what's in front of us right now and use what resources we have. Others will come.

It's also useful to do periodic reality checks. Where are you really? Everything has to be based on real results. Not an imaginary place in your head.

To a pioneering spirit who
was discouraged by frequent
criticism the Master said,
"Listen to the words of the
critic. He reveals what your
friends hide from you."
But he also said,
"Do not be weighed down
by what the critic says.
No statue was ever erected
to honour a critic.
Statues are for the criticized."

Anthony de Mello

How To Deal With Criticism

If you think for yourself, and act for yourself, the fact is you will be criticised.

Because you will not be like most people. Anyone who has ever achieved anything worthwhile has been criticised.

Look at any criticism objectively. There may be some truth and some learnings to be had. But when you've looked at it, discard it. It's bad enough things can be said to you once without playing things over and over continuously in your head.

Realise also, that today's heroes were yesterday's lunatics. They tried to put the Wright Brothers in a psychiatric hospital for even thinking they could make something that was heavier than air fly. But the airplane changed the world forever.

Jesus was persecuted in his time. Now, millions revere him as the son of God. The list is endless. It's easy to be a sceptic. Being a sceptic requires no change. You just throw rocks of doubt. The world needs dreamers. They are the ones who can make the world change into a better place.

"Regardless of how you feel

inside, always try to

look like a winner.

Even if you are behind,

a sustained look of

control and confidence

can give you a mental edge

that results in victory."

Arthur Ashe

1943-1993

Professional Tennis Player

And the first African American ever selected
to the U.S. Davis Cup team.

DRESS FOR SUCCESS

The above title doesn't imply wearing the best clothes money can buy.

Dress for success means be aware of what you're projecting to the world. Are your shoulders back? Is your head held high? Are you walking around with a frown or a smile on your face?

This quote reminds us to not react if life is not exactly where we want it to be. The simple action of maintaining a look of control and confidence can have the most beneficial effect. Not only on ourselves, but also on the people around us.

Realise that you affect people by the way you behave. In a competitive event, you can use this to your advantage.

In life, it's useful for everyone.

"Begin to free yourself at once by doing all that is possible with the means you have, and as you proceed in this spirit the way will open for you to do more."

Robert Collier

Prolific Writer and Publisher

STARTING FROM WHERE YOU ARE

When it comes to pursuing dreams, you very often hear 'I'd love to do that but…'.

You have to start from where you are. It doesn't matter how 'bad' you think the situation is, you can change it.

If you want to get inspired, then read the biography of someone who has achieved what others considered to be the impossible.

Don't fall into the trap of using your current life situation as an excuse for not doing things. To live with passion means living with what you have.

Sure we can all have our little moans. That's okay. Vent it, then move on.

Do all you can with what you have and pretty soon you'll find doors will start opening for you.

"Often the difference between a successful man and a failure is not one's better abilities or ideas, but the courage that one has to bet on his ideas, to take a calculated risk and to act."

Dr. Maxwell Maltz

Author of "Psycho-Cybernetics"

HAVING BALLS

Everyone needs to have balls. Women included. Certainly it seems that today, women can have more balls than a lot of men!

The courage to act and keep taking action until a successful outcome is reached, really comes from how much you believe you can have what you desire.

Very often, talent or skill is not the primary reason for success. It's wanting it badly. This drives what others call courage.

To the successful person, it's not courage. It's just another step towards their goal – which they can see, hear, feel and taste.

Think about why you should have this goal. What benefits will it bring you and others? Think about that and then go again!

INSPIRE ME

YOUR GOOD HEALTH

The foundation to a great life 157

Educate yourself 159

Healthy mind, healthy... 161

You have to maintain it 163

You control what you eat 165

Huge selection...not so good 167

This is key 169

Food for your brain 171

Move your body! 173

Supercharge materials 175

"He who enjoys
good health is rich,
though he knows it not."

Italian Proverb

THE FOUNDATION TO A GREAT LIFE

To enjoy all of the amazing things this world has to offer, your good health is a basic necessity.

It's only when we get ill that we realise how much we take for granted. We just expect our bodies to go on and on, regardless of what we do to them. In many ways, people take better care of their cars than their own bodies!

Having good health means looking after every level of being a human. That is, the three key areas - physical, mental and spiritual. Each of these is influenced by the other and each needs their own attention.

Your body and mind are amazing tools, but like a computer they need to be protected. Otherwise the smallest virus can cause a problem that hampers performance or worse still, shuts everything down.

To enjoy life, your good health should be a priority. So it's worth spending time and money finding out what works best for you. And base everything on what results it gives you.

"The doctor of the future
will give no medicine
but will interest their patients
in the care of the human
frame, in diet and in
the cause and prevention
of disease."

Thomas A. Edison

EDUCATE YOURSELF...

We live in an amazing time. Our daily choice of food is so vast in the Western world, it means we can get our hands on almost anything we want at any time of the day.

So why then, are so many adults and children overweight and obese? Why do so many people have diabetes? Why are brain degenerative diseases like Alzheimer's and Parkinson's on the increase?

If the results people are getting are not what they want (and who wants the above?), then it could be worth considering why we eat the way we do and the way we live.

We live in a time when we can get our hands on any information almost instantly. But there is so much out there, it's easy to get confused as to what's 'best' for you. Where do you start?

The first step is to make a decision. Decide you will take control of your health education. Then begin educating yourself on health and nutrition for the body and mind. Take an interest in prevention rather than cure. In the long term this will pay dividends.

"Mens sana in corpore sano"

Translation –

"A healthy mind in a healthy body"

HEALTHY MIND, HEALTHY...

The Greeks and Romans knew instinctively what science is only proving now. That is, your mind and your body are intrinsically linked. When you do something to the body, it affects your mind and vice versa.

So, if you exercise your body, it has a positive effect on your mind. Similarly, if you drink or eat something the body doesn't like, it can hamper performance of the brain. Similarly, if you're stressed in your mind, it can affect the body physically, through ulcers, tension and other side effects.

On the positive side, researchers have shown that when you visualise or imagine anything it has an immediate effect in the body. This could range from imaging something positive in the future or even practising a specific sporting exercise.

They've even shown that visualising yourself training in the gym helps increase muscle tone and strength! Couch potatoes will love that one!

Mental and physical health are linked. Both areas need your attention.

"Fitness -

If it came in a bottle,

everybody would have

a great body."

Cher

You Have To Maintain It

Have you ever noticed how a lot of people expect things NOW? The problem with living in a time that demands everything to be instant, is that when it comes to ourselves, we expect the same thing.

"I want to look great by eating anything, drinking anything and doing nothing!"

Well, unfortunately, the universal laws of life don't work that way. You have to sow something before you can reap it.

To get genuine good health, you can't just buy it in a bottle. It's a life long pursuit. It's a habit.

And like all habits. Once you practice it and keep at it, at some point it kicks in and becomes effortless, so that you don't have to think about it anymore.

A health body comes from healthy cells. Healthy cells come from a relaxed mind, good nutrition and proper exercise.

The practice of health in your life needs consistent attention.

"To eat is a necessity,

but to eat intelligently

is an art."

La Rochefoucauld

A clever French dude.

You Control
What You Eat

Eat what you like. Really.

Just be aware that different foods affect your body in different ways. It pays to educate yourself on how various foods impact you, because some can really cause damage to your body in the short and long term. As the quote says, it's essential to eat. But to eat in a way that positively affects you requires some education. Some learning.

If you put diesel into an unleaded car, it's going to cause a problem. Your body is the same. The problem might not be as immediate, but it will materialise at some point.

You don't need to know exactly how a car works to use it. But it is helpful to know some of the basics. In a similar way, you don't need to have a PhD in nutrition to know the basics of how your body works.

Make it your business to find out the basics of health. Just make sure the information you get, gives you the results you want.

"I'm on a seafood diet.
I see food and I eat it."

Author Unknown

HUGE SELECTION...
NOT SO GOOD.

The 'see' food diet mentioned on the far page is the kind of diet a lot of people are on. They eat whatever is in front of them, which is not the end of the world. But every action has a result and research is showing that different foods affect our bodies in different ways.

Sugars for one, have a very specific negative effects on our bodies. As do certain fats. The key is trusted information and results.

Many do not see the connection between good health and nutrition. Simple changes in your food habits can reduce the likelihood of you suffering illness. They can also positively affect your energy levels, moods and outlook.

Conventional medicine very often focuses on a short term solution that only treats the symptoms of a disease. But the cause can usually be traced back to poor diet or high levels of stress.

Your body is your machine. Maybe you should educate yourself on what fuel is best for it and why.

"This art of resting the mind and the power of dismissing from it all care and worry is probably one of the secrets of energy in our great men."

Captain J.A. Hadfield

THIS IS KEY

Instinctively, we know that being relaxed is a good thing.

But life can get so busy, that we can forget what 'relaxed' feels like until we're on holidays.

Being relaxed is your natural state. You're born that way. Relaxing or resting your mind regularly has huge benefits. Physical and mental.

Physically, your body improves its key functions. Your immune system gets a boost, and your vital organs perform better. Mentally, it's been proven you use more of your mind when you relax. You also become more creative and you definitely feel happier!

And as the words opposite point out, one of the greatest benefits is that you recharge the batteries and boost your energy levels.

Learning to relax regularly is simple, but it takes practice to make it a habit.

(Check out books and material by Herbert Benson, MD, Associate Professor Of Medicine at Harvard Medical School.)

"No diet will remove all the fat from your body because the brain is entirely fat. Without a brain, you might look good, but all you could do is run for public office."

George Bernard Shaw

FOOD FOR YOUR BRAIN

I wonder how many people know that your brain is 70% fat? Your brain responds instantly to the fuel received in your body. Your brain needs fat. 'Good' fat. And the fat it most needs is so-called omega-3. Without it, your brain cannot function at its top level.

Wonder food for the brain is wild fish rich in omega 3 oils. Particularly wild salmon, mackerel, herring and sardines. (Farmed fish doesn't have the same levels of omega 3).

If you don't like eating fish, you can always take supplements. Omega 3 oils have been shown to have a positive effect on things like:

Intelligence
Reduced inflammation in the blood
Skin and hair condition
Brain performance and health
Improves mood

One part of fish oil, called DHA, has been shown to enhance brain power, memory, and learning and may even prevent and possibly treat Alzheimer's disease.

"Those who do not find time for exercise will have to find time for illness."

Earl of Derby

MOVE YOUR BODY!

Some of my friends are blessed. They seem to eat and drink whatever they like, never exercise and yet they never put on weight!

This might be everyone's dream but my friends are actually worse off! They've really been spoiled with their body and genes. But because they 'get it' easy, they haven't had a reason to create good health. They may look good physically, but are they really healthy?

Think of it like the most expensive and sought after car in the world. It's common sense that if you just shine and clean the outside, yet neglect the mechanics of the engine, eventually something somewhere will go wrong. And the longer you leave it, the more likely it is that when a problem does emerge, it's usually something big.

Strangely, most people are nicer to their cars than they are to their bodies. And they wonder why, years down the line, it eventually breaks down. Avoid this trap. Start by doing anything. Just move your body! It's a living organism that needs it.

*"Whether you are young,
old, or in between, taking
vitamin-mineral supplements can
improve brain function, possible
boost performance on IQ tests,
improve mood and memory,
and slash the chances of brain
deterioration as you get older.
Indeed the evidence is
so compelling that is seems
incredible everyone is not taking
vitamins, minerals, and anti-oxidants
to keep their brains functioning at
peak levels for a lifetime."*

Jean Carper
Author of *'Your Miracle Brain'*
(Read This Book!)

SUPERCHARGE
MATERIALS

"**A** proper diet gives me all the nutrition I need."

My mother and my doctor used to say this to me
when I was a kid. While it may have been true years
ago, it sure isn't anymore. But I still hear people
saying it. (I'm not even sure it was true years ago!)
Research clearly shows that the modern Western
diet is lacking in some key essential nutrients and
vitamins. This is mostly due to the way foods are
grown, processed and eventually cooked. What's
more alarming relates to the quote opposite.
There is compelling evidence for everyone to be
taking supplements to bring their bodies back into
balance.

The good news is that these supplements are
readily available. The most vital are things like fish
oils, amino acids and anti-oxidants.

It doesn't mean that you need to be on the NASA
space programme and have 'pills' for everything.
Just start taking control of your own eating patterns.

Simple supplements can have massive effects on
your energy, your concentration, your mood and
your zest for life! We all want these!

INSPIRE ME

CHAPTER 9

LOVE & RELATIONSHIPS

The value of love   179

Jealousy. A dangerous thing   181

The greatest gift for kids   183

Don't allow recklessness   185

The best memories of your life   187

What women look for in men   189

What men look for in women   191

What you think, affects your relationships   193

The key to great relationships   195

Fuelling successful relationships   197

"Those who love deeply
never grow old;
they may die of old age,
but they die young."

Benjamin Franklin

1706-1790

Scientist, Publisher and Diplomat

THE VALUE OF LOVE

Love is a state of mind and a state of being. It's easy to assume that you can only find true love with another person. But that's not so. True love starts with yourself. Being comfortable in your own skin. Valuing yourself and really appreciating who you are.

Hollywood movies haven't done any favours in this regard. 'When you find that special someone, then it all changes.'

I believe there is someone for everyone, but true love will only blossom when both are in tune with themselves first. Those who are in love with themselves (in a non-ego way!) are in love with life. They enjoy and appreciate everything. That is the attitude that creates the 'young at heart' mindset.

Sigmund Freud said that unless the personality has love, it sickens and dies. Love is vital. Love is wishing for everyone, what you wish for yourself. It includes respect, goodwill, peace of mind and health.

The more love you give out, the more love comes back to. That's a law of life.

*"My wife's jealousy
is getting ridiculous.
The other day she looked
at my calendar and wanted
to know who May was."*

Rodney Dangerfield
American comedian and actor

JEALOUSY.
A DANGEROUS
THING.

A previous girlfriend of mine used to go out of her way to attract the attention of other men. At the time it used to drive me nuts! It sparked many a fight. But when I look back, I realise that my jealousy was a result of insecurities within myself. I didn't really value me. How great I was and am.

My jealousy said 'I'm afraid I'm not good enough and you might leave me.' For a man, in particular that's not a great thing to have in your head!

Ultimately, it was a good thing because the situations highlighted something within me.

It took several years to fully realise this lesson, but I did. And as a result I changed it and then started to attract a different type of woman. One who was more comfortable in herself and less inclined to play games.

The same law can apply to women too. The point is that 'negative' behaviour like jealousy springs from something within you.

Look within. Therein lies the answer.

"The greatest gift you and your partner can give your children is the example of an intimate, healthy, and loving relationship."

Barbara DeAngelis

Author

THE GREATEST GIFT FOR CHILDREN

You may decide to have kids or you may not. The point here is that the world needs great role models in relationships. We generally hear more about relationships breaking up than about how the great ones work.

Even, now there is still nothing taught in schools about relationships. We prefer to spend time teaching things that will mostly be of no value to a child when they become an adult.

We see a celebrity couple in 'love' and think 'they have it all', only to see the same couple a few years later breaking up with 'irreconcilable differences.'

Divorce and separation are on the increase. Children are growing up in a world where they may not believe a healthy relationship is possible. 'Relationship' is almost becoming a 'dirty' word.

Society needs role models for successful healthy relationships. And we need to study them to learn what makes the difference. This should then be taught to everyone. Understanding leads to awareness.

"Don't be reckless with other people's hearts, and don't put up with people that are reckless with yours."

Kurt Vonnegut, Jr.
American Novelist

DON'T ALLOW RECKLESSNESS

It's important to have standards. Seek out people who live lives that impress you and you will find that they will not tolerate certain things. From themselves or from others. They are very clear on their own standards.

When it comes to other people's hearts and your own, the same standard should apply.

Be honest with others even though they may react with upset. Never play games with someone's emotions. And even if it means walking away from someone you're 'crazy' about, because they're messing with your heart, do it knowing that you're doing the right thing.

Do what you believe to be the right thing, regardless of how the other person may react and it will always turn out right.

Always.

"The little unremembered acts of kindness and love are the best parts of a person's life."

William Wordsworth

Famous English Poet

THE BEST MEMORIES OF YOUR LIFE

Sit with someone over 80 years of age and ask them about their life. Ask what they remember with the most affection.

It's generally not the things they did with work or business (unless maybe they really did what they loved!). No, it's always about the people they knew, their loved ones, their friends and the things they did together.

They will remember the things others did for them. The kindness and love they gave and received. If they're lucky they will have lots of these kind of memories, and it will reflect in the level of sparkle in their eyes.

But, if they had little of this in their life, you will also see it in their face and eyes. Hardness, coldness, a lack of vitality.

I know which one I want!

What Women Look For In A Man...
Personality
Humour
Sensitivity
Brains
Good Body

What Men Think Women Look for...
Personality
Good body
Humour
Sensitivity
Good looks

*Taken from a survey of over 15,000 men
and women aged 17-60, to discover
what women and men are looking for in
a long-term sexual partner and what
each thinks the other wants.*

Source -

*'Why men can't listen and
why women can't read maps.'*
By Allan and Barbara Pease.

What Women Look For

This study reveals that men seem to be pretty much in touch with what a woman looks for in a man. But the 'good body' is lower on the women's list, which may surprise the men.

Women, in both a short-term and long term situation rank personality, humour and sensitivity as the main traits they look for. A good body is not a 'deal breaker.'

15% of the men in this study believed that having a large penis was important to women. But only 2% of women said it actually mattered. Maybe a lot of men reading this are now breathing a sigh of relief!

So regardless of what you think, the research is worth considering. Women value a good personality as the top quality in a man. Specifically, that means confidence, comfortableness in own skin and someone they can get on with.

That's why some men are very attractive to all women. They are relaxed with themselves and by default with everyone else.

What Men Look For In Women...
Personality
Good looks
Brains
Humour
Good Body

What Women Think Men Look for...
Good looks
Good body
Breasts
Bum
Personality

*Taken from a survey of over 15,000 men
and women aged 17-60, to discover
what women and men are looking for in
a long-term sexual partner and what
each thinks the other wants.*

Source -

*'Why men can't listen and
why women can't read maps.'*

By Allan and Barbara Pease.

WHAT MEN LOOK FOR

If you've read the previous page, you'll realise by looking at the answers opposite that women are not as in touch with the qualities they think men are looking for in a long term partner.

Of course it's understandable. Their answers are based on what they see men looking at, and what they hear them talking about. The media doesn't help either projecting images of how women should look to be attractive.

The 'What women think men want' list has some truth only when a man meets a woman for the first time. But these 'criteria' go way down the list when he is looking for a long term partner.

Again, personality is number 1.

"Just as animals are able to pick up fear vibration, many people are just as sensitive. The thoughts you believe are hidden are actually broadcast by your voice, your facial expressions, and your body language."

Taken from
'The Power Of Your Subconscious Mind'
By Joseph Murphy Ph D., D.D

WHAT YOU THINK AFFECTS YOUR RELATIONSHIPS

Think about it. You know instinctively if someone doesn't like you. They don't have to say it. You just pick it up. Realise that this also works when you're thinking certain things about people. And they react to it!

Likewise, you know when someone really likes or loves you. Their voice, face and body language say it all. Just be aware, that this all starts with just how a person is thinking. They don't have to say a word!

Very often we can play scenes in our minds about the past or future. Maybe we're suspicious that our loved one is having an affair. It may or may not be true but once we start to focus on it, our bodies react to it and the other person picks up on it.

When we meet our loved one, our thinking has been coloured and we're looking for clues to validate our suspicions. Remove these thoughts and replace with ones of harmony and love. When you meet the person you will have a completely different meeting.

"All things whatsoever

ye would that men should

do unto you,

do ye even so to them"

MATT. 7:1-2

From The Bible

THE KEY TO GREAT RELATIONSHIPS

Your unconscious mind is like a very sensitive recording machine. It's listening all the time and it plays back in your life what you record on it. So when it comes to relationships, and I'm not just talking about intimate ones, be very careful what you think! For example, you may be really 'nice' to someone but when their back is turned you are very critical in your mind. Be warned that this is like taking poison... into your body! Your unconscious mind responds and it will reflect in your body, your attitudes and even your moods.

It may even help attract situations to validate what you've been thinking. Is everyone against you? Then, think about who you are against in your mind? What have you been saying to yourself about people?

Think about this. Everyone knows someone who everyone loves. This type of person is someone who only thinks the best of people regardless of what others may see. As a result, everyone loves them.

Your thoughts are creative. In a nutshell, the key to great relationships is to wish for the other what you wish for yourself.

'There is more hunger
for love and appreciation
in this world than for bread.'

Mother Teresa

FUELING SUCCESSFUL RELATIONSHIPS

Everyone wants to be loved and appreciated. Everyone wants to feel important. Pride is a very important part of people's make up. If you can remember this for all of your relationships, it will guide you well.

It's easy to take the people around you for granted. Your loved ones. Your employees. Your employer or business partner. Your friends.

Yet they, like you, want to be recognised and appreciated. Very often we can ignore what they do for us.

The fuel to all successful relationships is genuine love and appreciation.

Expressed often.

INSPIRE ME

CHAPTER 10

MONEY AND WEALTH

We need to understand money   201

Money and happiness   203

Branson's quick way to being a millionaire 205

It's the way you use it…   207

A secret of the rich   209

Waiting for that windfall   211

The cost of pleasure…   213

Giving money to charity   215

A by-product of playing   217

Life's wages   219

"I'd say it's been my biggest
problem all my life...
it's money. It takes a lot of
money to make
these dreams come true."

Walt Disney

We Need To Understand Money

Money is important in today's world. But like everything, it can be used for great things or it can be used selfishly.

The reality is that like all art forms, the art of making and growing money requires a certain skill level.

The majority of people are not financially intelligent. They might be very good at spending money but they are not that good at managing it or making it grow.

You don't need to be an expert with money but you do need to have a working knowledge of it.

It's a basic life skill. When you have it, you can get more things done in the world. So seek out ways to develop your understanding of money and if needs be, be prepared to pay well for good advice.

This quote from a man who was considered very wealthy.

"All I ask is the chance

to prove that money

can't make me happy."

Spike Milligan.

MONEY AND HAPPINESS

My mother used to say to me 'Money can't make you happy.' And she was right, but...

...people who don't have money probably don't believe it.

Sigmund Freud, the famous psychologist, used to say he'd prefer to work with the rich rather than the poor because 'the rich know that money isn't everything!'

Despite this, I don't know anyone who'd refuse the chance that Spike Milligan asked for. And it's a funny thing... people who don't have a lot of money seem to delight in hearing that someone with a lot of money has an unhappy life or had a bit of misfortune. It almost justifies why they don't have money!

The reality of course, is that it is better to be happy than rich. But there is no harm in being both! You are entitled to have both and they are not mutually exclusive. Money and happiness can go hand in hand!

"What's the quickest way
to become a millionaire?
Borrow fivers off
everyone you meet."

Richard Branson

Branson's Quick Way To Being A Millionaire...

We live in an age of making a quick buck.

People are obsessed with making lots of money with little work. Certainly we live in a time when it's easier to make money than ever before and more millionaires are being created than ever before.

But there is no such thing as earning wealth through a lack of work. The only place where success comes before work is in the dictionary.

I love the comment by Ted Turner on becoming a millionaire. 'Don't become one for the money', he said, 'become one for the person it makes you become.'

There is no such thing as an overnight success. Yes, you can go from zero to hero overnight, but what many often ignore is the work and commitment that has gone before success arrives.

Even Branson's suggestion will take some time...

"Capital as such is not evil;
it is its wrong use that is evil.
Capital in some form or other
will always be needed."

Mohandas K. Gandhi

IT'S THE WAY YOU USE IT...

'Money is the root of all evil.' Statements like this haven't helped with the perception that money is a 'bad' thing.

Capitalists are often seen as 'wrong' doers. Yet people who have made money through their businesses and ideas very often change the world and our quality of lives in the process.

Can that be said to be a 'bad' thing?

Air travel, the motor cars, computers, television, telephones, to name a few, have transformed the world we live in. They have made our lives better.

The companies behind these have also employed people all over the world allowing their quality of life to be raised.

Yes, people have exploited our world's resources and our neighbours. Yes, the use of some money has been evil but it's up to you to correct that.

And yes. One person can make a difference and it's never too late to start.

"The poor and the middle
class work for money.
The rich have money
work for them"

Rich Dad

Source: *'Rich Dad, Poor Dad'*,
by Robert T. Kiyosaki

A Secret Of The Rich

People all over the world are waking up to the fact that there are options when it comes to their work.

The majority of people have been prisoners within the system of work. Daily slogging at jobs that they don't enjoy or get little thanks for.

Surely there is more to life than this?

'If only I had more money, I'd love to do my own thing.' The good news is that there are now more ways than ever to step outside the system and do more of what you love to do.

The rich are that way because of how they use money. And one of the basic secrets is making money work for you.

Understanding how to do this is no longer a secret. There are many sources to help learn the secrets of the rich. The program quoted opposite is one possible one.

Apply the secrets step by step and most of all…be patient. (but not too patient!)

"If God only gave me
a clear sign; like making
a large deposit in my name
at a Swiss bank."

Woody Allen

WAITING FOR THAT WINDFALL

As you go through life, you will observe two types of people. Those that wait for things to happen and those that act, and make things happen.

Some say 'When the time is right, then I'll do it.' Or 'If I visualise it and keep asking God for it, then it'll come.' Or maybe 'When I win the lottery…'.

Rewards come to those who act. Signs come to those who move. Start now with where you are. Take one step and the next one will reveal itself.

Thinking of writing that book? Write the first page. Then the next. Talk to someone who has done what you want to do. Do something!

But remember, don't put off living 'until you get there'. None of us know when we will leave this world and we can get caught up to such a degree with achieving things that we forget to appreciate the things that money can't buy.

"It is good to have money
and the things that money
can buy, but it's good too,
to check up once in a while
and make sure you haven't
lost the things
money can't buy."

George Lorimer

1867-1937

Editor of *"Saturday Evening Post"*

THE COST OF PLEASURE...

During a period of my life when I was caught up with earning a living, as opposed to just living, a wise man offered me a piece of advice.

'Take a blank page and list down your top 50 favourite fun things to do. Then beside each one note whether they cost anything to do and if so, how much.' I've never forgotten this simple task because of what I discovered.

Of my list of 50 fun things to do, 35 of them cost nothing. They only involved my time. Things like walking on the beach, playing the guitar or spending time with family and friends. And the remaining 15 items had very low costs attached to them.

Until I completed this exercise, I was putting off living 'until I had x amount of money'. But all the while, life was passing me by. At the time, I was doing very few of the things on the list.

From that point on, I resolved to look at that list every week and pick a number of fun things to do. The interesting thing, was that the list over time started to grow...

"Let us not be satisfied with just giving money. Money is not enough, money can be got, but they need your hearts to love them. So, spread your love everywhere you go."

Mother Teresa

Giving Money To Charity

Giving money to charity is something many people do. Here's a point to consider though.

Sometimes giving money is the easiest thing to do. A friend from Africa once remarked to me that 'giving money to help the babies in Africa is akin to me giving money to help the white drug addicts in Dublin.'

His point was not that it's wrong to try and help people in Africa but not to neglect the difference you can make in your own community.

Maybe we can ease our conscience by saying we give to charity. But maybe the question we should ask of ourselves is 'what can I do with my own unique blend of talents and skills that would enrich my community?'

We can be so concerned about changing the world that we forget about changing ourselves, our families or our community.

"Stop chasing the money

and start chasing the passion"

Tony Hsieh

Founder of Zappos.com

A BY-PRODUCT OF PLAYING

Any person who amasses a serious amount of wealth will usually say something like this. 'It's rarely about the money. It's about the fun, enjoyment, the buzz, the challenge or about providing a life changing service.'

In fact, anyone who is successful in any field could say something similar.

The success lies in the doing. When you're focused on what you're doing and not about what you're going to get then you ignite the fire of your potential.

Do what you love to do. Money will come. I know a talented artist who earns a good living, doing what she loves. She expects to make money. She is often amazed at other talented artists who only scrape by.

Because she is passionate about what she does. This drives her to get better, to take risks and to move towards her goals. And people pick up on it.

Keep passion and enjoyment in your life and if it's not there, keep changing until you get it.

Life's Wages
by Author Unknown

I bargained with Life for a penny,
And Life would pay no more
However I begged at evening
When I counted my scanty store.

For Life is a just employer
He gives you what you ask,
But once you have set the wages,
Why, you must bear the task.

I worked for a menial's hire
Only to learn, dismayed,
That any wage I had asked of Life,
Life would have willingly paid.

Source:

'Think and Grow Rich'

LIFE'S WAGES

True wealth is not measured in monetary terms, but it's no harm having money. You can do lots of good with it.

Even if you don't want it for yourself, you can earn a lot and give it away to others who need it.

Just remember that the starting point for earning money is always in your mind. Your mind 'tells' you what you're worth.

But what has been shown is that you can now train your mind to expect what you want. You decide your worth.

Visualisation plays a huge part in this, as the mind does not know the difference between what's real and what's imagined.

It doesn't mean there will be changes overnight, but there will be changes.

When you boil water, it takes some time for the steam to appear. You could be fooled into thinking nothing was happening...

CHAPTER 11

SUCCEEDING AT BUSINESS

The most important quality...   223

The key to success in business...   225

The smartest business person...   227

How to save time and money...   229

Master this art to stand out...   231

Getting your worth...   233

How to get the best from people...   235

Take experience over cash...   237

How to get inspiration...   239

How to convince people...   241

"It takes 20 years to build a reputation and five minutes to ruin it. If you think about that, you'll do things differently."

Warren Buffett

Investment Entrepreneur

At the time of writing this book,
Warren Buffett is ranked by Forbes as the
3rd richest person in the world, with an estimated
net worth of $42 billion. (behind only Bill Gates).
What's more interesting is that he has pledged
to give 85% of his wealth to charitable causes,
with 'The Bill and Melinda Gates' Foundation'
being the main beneficiary. This is the largest
charitable act in the United States history.

THE MOST IMPORTANT QUALITY...

The future of business is going to be centred around relationships built on integrity and trust.

In a world that has exposed so many for a lack of integrity, anyone who can maintain that quality, genuinely, will go far.

Good business is built on successful relationships. People buy from people they trust and like. When you're honest and straight with people, and put their needs first, you will always stand out from the crowd.

The quote on the far page reminds us that we will always be tested. You can spend a lifetime doing the right thing, only to lose your reputation by making one bad choice decision.

Be true to your self. Even in the face of others trying to sway you. If you are always true to your self, you won't go wrong. Do the right thing consistently, and you will become a person that is admired and respected.

Believe in yourself and stand for your personal values.

"The man who works
merely because he has to,
will never advance."

Anon

THE KEY TO SUCCESS IN BUSINESS...

The world needs passion. Passion comes from doing the things you love to do.

All successful business people have one thing in common. They love what they do. That's one of the reasons they get ahead. They are so passionate that they will persist where others stop.

Business can be challenging enough without doing something you don't enjoy.

Some people know instinctively what they love to do. Some people don't. If you're in the latter category, the way to find your passion is to start with the things you like. Keep experimenting until you discover the career, profession or business you were born to be in.

Even if you're not there yet, start in your spare time. Or whatever time. If nothing else, at least you'll increase your level of fulfilment in life.

And remember, if you keep looking, you will find it!

"The best executive is the
one who has sense enough
to pick good men to do
what he wants done,
and self-restraint to keep
from meddling with
them while they do it."

Theodore Roosevelt.

THE SMARTEST BUSINESS PERSON...

The smartest business person of all is one that hires people that are smarter than them and can then leave them to get on with the job. You don't have to have the highest IQ, or have the most qualifications to run a successful team or company. Many great companies have been owned by men and women who knew they didn't know it all. Richard Branson being one example. But what they did know is the importance of having the right people around them. This is a trait that all great leaders have.

If you want to get on in business, you have to know how people work. To get the best from a person, you need to know how to motivate them, how to lead them, and how to inspire them.

Learn from others. Learn by diving in. Learn by any means possible. And most of all, learn from your own mistakes.

If you can master the art of finding good people and have them work for you willingly, you will have cracked one of the most important secrets to being wealthy, successful and fulfilled.

"Get good counsel
before you begin
and when you have decided,
act promptly."

Salhurst

How To Save Time And Money...

Why re-invent the wheel? There are people out there who will have done or most likely tried some part of what you're about to do. Some may have succeeded, others may have failed. You can learn from both.

Digest their nuggets of wisdom, decide which ones you want to learn from and then take action. The most important thing is to keep moving.

Many people get the advice, make a plan and then stop. They might be busy, but very often it's busy doing the 'wrong' thing.

Be ruthless with yourself. Ask yourself these questions. What is the best use of my time right now? And, is what I'm doing right now moving me in the direction of my goals?

Then most importantly act promptly on the answers.

"You look at any giant
corporation, and I mean
the biggies, and they all
started with a guy
with an idea, doing it well."

Irvine Robbins

Co-Founder of Baskin-Robbins Ice Cream

MASTER THIS ART TO STAND OUT...

The difference between success and failure lies in the doing.

Einstein said that genius was '1% inspiration and 99% perspiration.' Ideas visit everyone. Unfortunately, few act on them.

Even if you partner with someone in business who is high on the action front, you'll still benefit in your life by cultivating the habit of taking action.

The other side of the coin is acting on too many ideas, to the extent that none of them get finished! This can be the curse of many an entrepreneur.

Take one idea and implement it. Fully. Do this and you will do more than most people ever do. Let that completed idea be your springboard to the next one.

"It's unwise to pay too much,
but it's worse to pay too little.
When you pay too much, you lose a
little money - that is all.
When you pay too little, you
sometimes lose everything
because the thing that you bought
was incapable of doing the
things it was bought for.
The common law of business
balance prohibits paying a little
and getting a lot - it can't be done.
If you deal with the lowest bidder,
it is well to add something for the
risk you run, and if you do that, you
will have enough to pay
for something better."

John Ruskin

1819 - 1900

GETTING YOUR WORTH...

If needs be, use the words on the far page when dealing with someone who wants what you're selling for less than the value you've placed on it. That includes you, say if it's for a new job (although be open to trading off money versus great experience)

The key however, is to ensure that what you're selling is of good quality, and that it does what you say it does. The best salespeople sell with integrity and are keen to build genuine long term relationships.

Of course, the same applies when you're buying. Remember, you get what you pay for. And despite the fact that everything is negotiable, to get the best, you have to pay for it. Just ensure that what you're paying for, is worth it. If needs be do your homework.

A simple principle but often forgotten.

"I consider my ability to
arouse enthusiasm among my
people the greatest asset I
possess, and the way
to develop the best that is
in a person is by appreciation
and encouragement."

Charles Schwab

How To Get The Best From People...

Most people are under appreciated and as a result, underperform.

The best companies in the world are those that recognise the potential in their staff and give them the means and encouragement to achieve it.

It's not all about money either. Simple words like 'Thank you' or 'Well done' can be the most motivating of all. Genuine appreciation given at the right time, can make all the difference to the people you are working with.

Realise that most of the people you will ever work with, don't see their full potential. And it's easy to unlock it. All you have to do is to recognise it and give encouragement where others give put downs.

Very often the person with average talent but great self-belief can achieve the impossible. That belief was probably sparked by someone who saw potential in them and helped draw it out. In this way, you can be the spark that ignites the fire of potential in people around you.

"In the business world,

everyone is paid in two coins:

cash and experience.

Take the experience first;

the cash will come later."

Harold S. Geneen

Accountant, Industrialist and CEO

TAKE EXPERIENCE OVER CASH

Most people want to be instant experts.

But the reality is that you will have to go through a period as an 'apprentice' in whatever your chosen field is.

Go after working with the best over working with the mediocre for better money. Even if it means working for free.

By working with the best, you will learn what makes them successful and in doing so, you increase your chances of achieving it yourself. They'll also save you a lot of time, as you can learn from their mistakes.

Some say that 2 years is a good apprentice time. You will have to be the judge of that yourself. Just be clear that people pay for results and by working with the best, you learn how to get the best results.

And once you know this, the money will come.

"Every now and then go away,
have a little relaxation, for
when you come back
to your work your judgment
will be surer. Go some
distance away because
then the work appears
smaller and more of it can be
taken in at a glance and a lack
of harmony and proportion
is more readily seen."

Leonardo Da Vinci
1452-1519
Inventor, Architect, Painter,
Scientist and Sculptor

How To Get Inspiration...

At the time of writing this book, the western world is at an important point in history.

People are realising that there is more to life than being in the 'rat race', yet they are still caught within the cult of 'hard work'. Many work long hours as they believe that they have to work them to succeed. But this can often be at the expense of relationships, health and life. But a revolution is occurring and many people are questioning the model of modern 'living.'

Business has the ability to consume your every waking thought. And there will always be more business to be done. Always.

When you next feel over consumed by business or even by life, step away, take a break and relax. Not just physically but mentally. Turn off your phone and go and do something you enjoy to take your mind off work. Have some fun!

You're guaranteed to get some insights when you return to your business later on.

"What convinces is conviction.
Believe in the argument you're
advancing. If you don't, you're
as good as dead.
The other person will sense
that something isn't there, and
no chain of reasoning,
no matter how logical or
elegant or brilliant,
will win your case for you."

Lyndon B. Johnson
1908-1973
Thirty-Sixth President of the United States

How To Convince People...

To believe in the argument you're advancing, as the quote opposite says, it's vital to do your homework. That is, do your research.

Whether it's a product you're selling, an idea you're promoting or maybe a colleague you're seeking to influence, the first person to convince is yourself. You need to believe in yourself and what you're saying.

Some people have the gift of sounding convincing, even though they may not be correct. This is more the skill of a charlatan and in time, they will be found out.

To sound convincing, you need to be convinced beyond doubt yourself. This requires spending time convincing yourself. (Convinced?)

Before you try to persuade anyone else, reflect on whether you've sold yourself. And if you haven't, fill in the gaps by doing your homework.

INSPIRE ME

CHAPTER 12

WHEN THINGS GO WRONG...

There really is no such thing as failure...   245

Everyone who is anyone has 'failed'   247

Mistakes are ESSENTIAL for success   249

Your goal is to learn from everything   251

Mistakes are the pathway to success   253

Persistence pays off   255

The worst fear of all   257

Have some stories to tell   259

The value of obstacles   261

Keep your eyes on the prize   263

"I am not discouraged,
because every wrong
attempt discarded
is another step forward."

Thomas Edison

Holds the record for the largest number
of patents registered even though
he had little formal education.

There Really Is No Such Thing As Failure...

There is only feedback!

Society has conditioned us to see making mistakes as a 'bad' thing. So much so that children and adults can be paralysed with the fear of failure.

If you want to get on in anything, you have to make mistakes. That's how we learn as humans. We learn by trial and error. It's how we learned to walk, ride a bicycle, drive a car.

Anyone who has ever been recognised as a great in their field, has made huge mistakes. Imagine if Edison had given up after a 100 times of trying to invent the light bulb! In the end it took him over 10,000 tests to finally get it right.

He didn't recognise failure. He saw every attempt as a step forward because he learned from it. He took the feedback, made changes and then had another go.

Maybe there's somewhere in your life where you can apply the same mindset...

"No man ever achieved
worthwhile success who
did not, at one time or other,
find himself with at least
one foot hanging well
over the brink of failure."

Napoleon Hill,
American Speaker, Motivational Writer,
"Think and Grow Rich"

Everyone Who Is Anyone Has 'Failed'

The word failure can be dangerous, because so much seems to be associated with it.

It almost seems to imply 'The End'. It's one thing for others to think this of you; it's a far more serious thing for you to see yourself as a 'failure'.

If we can adopt the mindset of seeing every event as a learning experience, and at the same time keep our ultimate goal in mind, we will achieve far more than we ever dreamed. The only limit is your imagination.

Where would the world be without the dreamers and those unafraid to take risks and learn from their mistakes?

When we look at people we deem 'successful', we often only see what they've done. Not what they've had to overcome. And they've all made 'mistakes'. Some whoppers too.

"If you don't have failures, you

aren't doing.

And if you aren't doing,

you can't have success."

Lewis Lehr

Former Chairman of 3M Corporation,
creators of the 'Post-It'
and other innovative products.

MISTAKES ARE ESSENTIAL FOR SUCCESS

3M is recognised as being one of the most creative and inventive companies in the world.

Creators of the 'Post-It' and countless other useful inventions, this quote by a former chairman is quite telling.

It's rare to get it right first time. Particularly if it's something new. 3M encourage making mistakes. Could that be why they come up with so many innovative products?

Sometimes the greatest discovery can result from a mistake. The main thing is to keep taking action. To keep learning.

And if you want to succeed at a faster rate, then you have to be prepared to make more mistakes.

Of course, you do have to learn from them. And when you do, your success rate takes off.

"A man's errors are

his portals of discovery."

James Joyce

YOUR GOAL IS TO LEARN FROM EVERYTHING

If you can adopt this mindset to life, it will have an amazing effect on you.

Most people expect to succeed or win on the first go. At the very least people expect to get better with every try. That's not life and this expectation is largely because of the way we are conditioned by society.

If you say 'Ok, my goal here is to learn with every attempt', the effect on your esteem and self-confidence is dramatically different.

It takes the pressure off. Your mind becomes focused on learning and improving instead of fear of failure. It starts to focus on the act of doing rather than worrying about failure.

That alone makes a huge difference.

Try it.

"Failure is in a sense
the highway to success,
in as much as every
discovery of what is false
leads us to seek earnestly
after what is true,
and every fresh experience
points out some form of error
which we shall afterward
carefully avoid."

John Keats

MISTAKES ARE THE PATHWAY TO SUCCESS

When you look at every attempt as an opportunity to learn, then the fear is taken out of making mistakes.

Mistakes now become a part of getting to your goal. That's how we learn as humans anyway. Especially when we're kids. The danger is when you become an adult you can stop doing things for fear of making mistakes.

Mistakes are a part of the process of success!!! Ingrain that in your mind. Mistakes are a good thing because they help you learn.

That's why it very useful to stop and review your actions and results.

Regularly ask yourself what's working and what's not. Ask questions of your results and performance. Questions like 'What can I learn from this?' and 'How can I improve my performance?

"Most of the important things
in the world have been
accomplished by people
who have kept on trying
when there seemed to be
no help at all."

Dale Carnegie
1888-1955
Author and Trainer

PERSISTENCE PAYS OFF

You can be sure that everyone encounters days when it feels like 'it just isn't happening.'

Everyone has had moments when they've thought 'Maybe I'll just throw in the towel.'

The difference between success and not achieving your goal, is usually in the way you think.

Persistence comes from a state of mind that will not accept defeat. In other words, failure is not an option.

Most achievements have occurred because of people's single minded determination to make it happen.

They kept on and on, when it probably seemed illogical. But that's part of the secret of people who excel at getting on. They expect things to go 'wrong', but they learn and keep going until they get to their destination.

"Don't fear failure so much
that you refuse to try new
things. The saddest summary
of a life contains three
descriptions: could have,
might have, and should have."

Louis E. Boone

Author from United States

THE WORST FEAR OF ALL

Try everything. Even if you are not the greatest at it at first, just try it.

Where would we be if we never tried anything new?

We should never grow up when it comes to just doing things. It's a habit that should be cultivated in every school and business around the world.

Just do things. Don't think about it. Do it.

So what if you don't succeed first time? You can learn from it. You're still you!

Ask that girl or guy out! Try that parachute jump! Go for that dream job! Push yourself to do the things you fear. They are only psychological.

Be a dream maker, not a dream breaker!

"Far better is it to dare mighty things, to win glorious triumphs even though chequered by failure, than to rank with those poor spirits who neither enjoy nor suffer much because they live in the grey twilight that knows neither victory nor defeat."

Theodore Roosevelt
26th President of the United States

HAVE SOME
STORIES TO TELL

Wouldn't it be great to get to the end of your days on this planet, and be able to look back on your life with satisfaction?

To know that you really gave it your all. Sure, maybe everything didn't go to plan – it never really does!

But you sure went for it. On every level. And most of all you encouraged other people to do the same. That is, you inspired and encouraged them to give things a go. To go for their dreams.

Wouldn't it be great to have lots of stories to tell about a life less ordinary. A life that was and is yours!

"Strength does not come from winning. Your struggles develop your strength. When you go through hardship and decide not to surrender, that is strength."

Arnold Schwarzenegger

Bodybuilder, Actor and Politician

THE VALUE OF OBSTACLES

Obstacles test you.

They test your resolve, your determination and your creativity.

A successful life is not one free of obstacles. It's one where obstacles are present but how they're handled and viewed is different from the average life.

Arnold Schwarzenegger has had major obstacles in his way at different parts of his life. But his attitude and mindset determined his level of success. A successful bodybuilder, Hollywood actor and politician, almost everything he has achieved most would have thought impossible, for a young boy from Austria.

Believe it or not, you learn the most, not when things are going right, but when things are going wrong! Because when you decide to succeed despite any setbacks, you find ways of making things work. You develop inner strength and in that way obstacles become your friends because they make you better.

"Obstacles cannot crush me,

every obstacle yields

to stern resolve. He who

is fixed to a star does not

change his mind."

Leonardo Da Vinci

1452-1519

Scientist, Inventor, Artist

i.e. the guy who painted the Mona Lisa

KEEP YOUR EYES ON THE PRIZE

Another expression for the prize is the big picture or goal. Everybody has moments when the clouds block the sun. When inspiration and motivation hit rock bottom.

The key to moving out of this is to:

Realise that it's a mental block

And

Revisit your big picture.

That is, use your imagination to experience what it will be like when you achieve your goal. What will you be doing? What impact will achieving your goal have on your life and others?

Ask yourself again, why are you pursuing this goal anyway? What was your original motivation? Write the answers down and digest them.

When you're crystal clear on your goal, and are committed to taking action, obstacles are nothing.

CHAPTER 13

OVERCOMING YOUR FEARS

Fear is dangerous   267

The enemy is fear   269

The solution to fear   271

Conquering fear   273

A waste of your time   275

This makes a big difference   277

Fear or faith?   279

Afraid of letting others down   281

How to be magnetic   283

Where to put your attention   285

Be wary of the words of others   287

"Fear defeats more people

than any other one thing

in the world."

Ralph Waldo Emerson

American author, poet and philosopher.
A guy with interesting things to say.

FEAR IS
DANGEROUS

I was once told that there are only 2 basic emotions in the world, and all other emotions come from these.

The 2 emotions are fear and love. In the case of fear, it can be the root cause of never trying something you've always wanted to do. It can be the source of anger and aggression. It can take the shape of many negative emotions.

One thing is certain, fear can stop you from living the best life you can. Very often it's the fear of failure or the fear of looking foolish that holds someone back from making that next important step in their lives.

It takes a very aware person to 'feel the fear and do it anyway'. But that is the way to conquering your fears.

Afraid of someone rejecting you? What's the worst that can happen?

Realise when you meet people, 99% of them have fears. You can grow that fear, or help kill it.

"The enemy is fear.

We think it is hate;

but, it is fear."

Gandhi.

Skinny bald guy who inspired a nation
by the power of his vision and mindset

THE ENEMY IS FEAR

Treat fear like the vilest virus known to man. Because it is. It can suck the life from people and stop us from having great lives.

Plus it's contagious. Speak to someone who is consumed with fear in any area of their lives and the energy dial gets turned to low and you probably won't feel as 'optimistic' about life as before.

So where you see it, stamp it out. Particularly in the young. Life can sometimes grow the fear monster within you. Kill it.

Kill it by doing the next point...

"Stand up to your obstacles

and do something about them.

You will find that they

haven't half the strength

you think they have."

Norman Vincent Peale

1898-1993

Pastor, Speaker and Author

THE SOLUTION TO FEAR

In a safari park in South Africa, I was lucky to spend some time with an experienced ranger. He told me of the most fearful moment in his life. He'd been out on foot in the jungle and unluckily had attracted the unwanted attention of a lion. Before he had time to think, the angry animal was charging towards him. My friend only had a split second to act and luckily for him his training kicked in. He didn't move. The king of the jungle was running at him and he managed to stand still. His heart was pumping and the voice in his head was screaming 'Run! Run!" But he stood his ground. The lion skidded in to within 3 feet of him and stopped. It gave a roar that shook the ground for a mile. My friend could see right into the animal's eyes and fierce mouth. Neither he nor the lion moved for several minutes.

Then, gradually over the next 2 hours he took 1 step back every 3 to 4 minutes until he was a safe distance away. He had faced the king of the jungle and lived to tell the tale. The ranger said 'We're trained not to run. If I had turned and tried to escape, the lion would have killed me. By facing up to it, it sends a signal that I am not afraid and so the lion does not attack.' Maybe there's something in that when it comes to your life.

"Do the thing you fear to do
and keep on doing it...
that is the quickest
and surest way ever yet
discovered to conquer fear."

Dale Carnegie

CONQUERING FEAR

It's all too easy to be busy in every area of your life except the one area that you really know you have to deal with.

Fear, if let, can distract you from taking steps forward. Afraid of speaking in public? Take the first step. Attend a speaking course. Go along to toastmasters. Ask a friend for mentoring. Start with something. Anything. And then keep going!

Take the first step and the next will appear. Pretty soon, you'll be like the small snowball rolling down the hill. You'll gradually gain momentum to a degree that you'll be unstoppable. And then you'll look back and wonder what all the fuss was about.

As you take action in the areas you fear you begin to realise that they were illusions of the mind. A subtle form of magic trickery that we play on ourselves. But it's not good magic.

If you can train yourself to take action and ignore the fear, you will have done something amazing.

You'll have conquered the dark side!

"The last of the human freedoms: to choose one's attitude in any given set of circumstances, to choose one's own way."

Viktor Frankl

1905-1997
Neurologist, Psychiatrist and Author.
He wrote *'Man's search for Meaning'*,
which is worth a read.

This Makes A Big Difference

Take two people of similar ability, and give them the same task to complete. Their results will always vary in relation to their attitudes. History shows us that despite unfortunate circumstances or experiences, men and women can succeed in any area of their lives. It all comes down to attitude.

Oprah Winfrey conquered poverty and a tragic childhood to become an inspiration to people all over the world. Edison invented the light bulb despite leaving school at the age of 12!

Look around you. There are people in every community that overcome hardship, defying logic.

My own brother was deaf in his left ear from birth and about 60% hearing in his right ear. Yet, his first job after leaving college was in tele-sales – the last place you'd think. And to top it all off, he was always in the top 2%.

He succeeded despite his physical limitation. His attitude has always amazed me and continues to inspire me. What's your attitude like today?

"It's a lack of faith
that makes people afraid
of meeting challenges,
and I believe in myself."

Muhammad Ali

A legend

Fear Or Faith?

Muhammad Ali continues to inspire men and women all over the world. No-one could ever accuse this man of not believing in himself, despite the fact that he has Parkinson's disease.

People can doubt so much in life. This doubt stems from fear. Fear of failure, fear of the unknown, fear of change.

When you are forced to go through a difficult time, you realise the potential you have. 'That which does not kill me makes me stronger.'

Take a blank page and write down a list of accomplishments you've done in the past 5 years. I guarantee you that there will be some things on that paper that at some point you never thought you could do.

We are too quick to focus on the things we didn't do. Focus on what you've done and you grow your self-belief.

By doing that, you grow your faith and eventually you'll be doing more of the 'impossible.'

"I can't tell you the key to
success but the
key to failure is trying to
please everyone."
- Ed Sheeran

Ed Sheeran

Singer - songwriter

Afraid Of Letting Others Down?

Every person in the world is a unique collage of beliefs, attitudes and experiences. For that reason, we will always have different ways of seeing the world. For 10 that agree with us, there will be 10 that will disagree. The key to success is for you to decide what success means to you and not allow yourself to be compromised.

It's important to ensure your values are true. Hitler knew what success meant for him, but his success was not good for the planet or humanity, and luckily for us he was stopped.

If success for you is living on a mountain top then do it. If success is not getting married then do it. The main thing is to live the way you wish. As a child growing up in Ireland the expression 'What will the neighbours think?' was thrown out occasionally when the option of doing something different came up. We can be so concerned about what others think that we forget to ask ourselves what's best for our souls. It's okay to do something for you!

In fact, it's essential for a healthy, balanced world.

"There is nothing strange about fear: no matter in what guise it presents itself it is something with which we are all so familiar that when a man appears who is without it we are at once enslaved by him."

Henry Miller

American Writer

How To Be Magnetic

We follow people who believe in a compelling vision of the future. That vision overshadows any fear they may have.

True leaders face their fears head on and keep going. This can be in politics, sport, business or the community.

We are drawn to people who say 'I know we can do this, despite the odds.' And often all it takes is one person to act as a catalyst for that potential to come out. It's not that great leaders don't have fears. They just move past them.

What can you do today to help inspire those around you? Is there a situation in your life where some vision and fearlessness is needed?

There's a clue in the vision part. The clearer the picture of the goal, the easier it is to pass it on. The easier it is to overshadow the fear.

You want to be magnetic? Learn to create a picture of the future, stick to it no matter what and watch miracles happen.

"Don't waste life in doubts and
fears; spend yourself on the
work before you, well assured
that the right performance of
this hour's duties will be the
best preparation for the hours
and ages that will follow it."

Ralph Waldo Emerson

WHERE TO PUT YOUR ATTENTION

How much time have you wasted in thinking fearful thoughts? All the things that might happen and probably never will…

It's kind of like thinking about going for that walk, or going to the gym. Or even opening that lap top to continue writing that book. Thinking about it but doing nothing.

Too much thinking about it can stop you doing it!

Jump in and start doing what has to be done. Do it NOW! Don't worry about the future. Deal with what's in front of you right now 100%. Do it the best you can. And then deal with the next thing 100%. And so on.

All the while knowing that what you're doing is preparing yourself for the next moment in the best possible way. This is such a simple strategy that you could ignore it. It's great because it works. Use it and pass it on!

As my granny used to say 'Worry gives a small thing a big shadow.' Don't waste your life lost in worry. Lose yourself in doing.

"If the world should blow itself
up, the last audible voice
would be that of an expert
saying it can't be done."

Peter Ustinov

Successful journalist, actor,
playwright and author.

BE WARY OF THE WORDS OF OTHERS

The history of the world is the history of people saying 'it can't be done' and then having to eat their words.

They said that about airplanes, about cars, about going to the moon, about building the golden gate bridge, about you losing weight, about you gaining weight, about making lots of money, about being spiritual and having money at the same time, about changing career or trying totally different careers, about finding the love of your life, regardless of age.

It's said about Richard Branson that if you tell him it can't be done, his eyes light up and he starts getting very interested in proving it can be done.

The words 'it can't be done' are too easy to say and they stem from ignorance and a lack of openness of mind.

Never let someone else's words fuel the fire of fear in you. Someone else's 'can't be done' can be your 'easily done.'

INSPIRE ME

CHAPTER 14

THE BIG PICTURE

A life of perfect means, but no meaning   289

What industry are you in?   291

Look after your own garden   293

True measure of success   295

We are not alone   297

WIIFM or WIIFTW?   299

Helping hand   301

Your world   303

You can change the world   305

How to make your BIG picture irresistible   307

"Ours is a society that has perfected its means yet neglected its meaning."

Albert Einstein

A Life Of Perfect Means, But No Meaning

We live in an age of miracles. New inventions continue to transform our world, yet we take them mostly for granted.

Yet despite all of our technological advances, have we really progressed as people? Could you say in some cases we've gone backwards? There seems to be less community. Less connection. Less purpose. Less meaning.

But something is happening. People are waking up and a revolution is cooking. We are starting to ask ourselves more meaningful questions.

Why am I here? What is my purpose? What can I contribute? Why is it that 4 billion out of 6 billion people on my planet are in poverty?

Technological miracles are great. But we need more human miracles. Purpose and meaning comes through harnessing your talents to benefit others.

Ask yourself, 'how can I improve the lives of others through my unique blend of talents?

The Master welcomed the advances
of technology, but was keenly aware
of its limitations.

When an industrialist asked him what his
occupation was, he replied,
"I'm in the people industry."

"And what, pray, would that be?"
said the industrialist.

"Take yourself," said the Master. "Your efforts
produce better things; mine, better people."

To his disciples he later said,
"The aim of life is the flowering of persons.
Nowadays people seem concerned mostly
with the perfectioning of things."

Anthony de Mello
A man with interesting thoughts on spirituality

WHAT INDUSTRY ARE YOU IN?

The above question is a common one to ask amongst business people.

But wouldn't it be an interesting world if everyone was in the people business? Genuinely.

If we all were, would we allow the starvation, poverty and trouble that exist in the world? Or closer to home, would we allow people to exist homeless on the streets?

Would we shut off the potential of our children? Would we stop thinking of what we can get and start focusing on what we can give?

The people business is not about recruitment or slave trading. It's about helping people to grow and achieve their true potential. To empower them to live the lives they wish, in harmony with everyone else.

"No matter what you've done for yourself or for humanity, if you can't look back on having given love and attention to your own family, what have you really accomplished?"

Lee Iacocca

Former Chairman of Chrysler

LOOK AFTER YOUR OWN GARDEN

I once knew a man who on the face of it, was a great man. He was a genius at raising money for charity.

But as I got to know him, I realised that he had a very large ego that wanted the recognition of been known to help charity. Behind the scenes, his personal life was in a shambles. His wife resented him and his kids seemed to hate him. It wasn't a life worth having and it taught me a couple of home truths.

True achievement doesn't have to mean making millions, creating inventions or selling millions of records. It usually starts closer to home. Who are the people closest to me that I love? How am I helping them? What difference am I making to them? What difference am I making to the people around me? We can all (especially men!) get caught up with changing the world or great achievement. A lot of this stems from our ego (again...mostly men!).

Look at your life like a garden. Is it full of weeds or flowers? What can you start doing today to take care of the flowers and increase their beauty?

"Always demanding the
best of oneself, living with
honour, devoting one's talents
and gifts to the benefits
of others - these are the
measures of success that
endure when material things
have passed away."

Gerald Ford

Former President of the United States

TRUE MEASURES
OF SUCCESS

Growing up in today's world can be confusing.
Especially when you're TOLD what success is.

But the reality of true success isn't always what you'll
see on TV, in magazines or hear about with friends.

Being the 'best' is different from demanding the best
from yourself. Everyone is a unique person and we
all have our own blend of unique talents. There is
no-one else like you in the world.   No-one.

Material success like money, cars, houses, looks,
clothes will all be gone when you move on. True
success is immortal – it lives on even when you
leave planet earth. What use is that you say?

Well the funny thing is…when you focus on using
your life to benefit others…your fulfilment levels rise
considerably.

But don't believe me. Just try it out and see. And
be aware of the next quote…

"Strange is our situation here upon earth. Each of us comes for a short visit, not knowing why, yet sometimes seeming to divine a purpose. From the standpoint of daily life, however, there is one thing we do know - we are here for the sake of each other, above all, for those upon whose smile and well-being our own happiness depends, and also for the countless unknown souls with whose fate we are connected by a bond of sympathy. Many times a day I realize how much my own outer and inner life is built upon the labours of others, both living and dead, and how earnestly I must exert myself in order to give in return as much as I have received and am still receiving."

Albert Einstein

WE ARE NOT ALONE…

The world you live in is the overall result of all the contributions from the human beings who have ever lived on the planet.

The food you are eating today didn't just magically appear. Many people helped put it there. The books educating you were created by someone who came before you. Our houses are lit at night because of Thomas Edison and his team. We have a lot to be thankful for from people we have never met. Einstein's comment shows us how grateful he felt. So much so, that he felt compelled to give back as much as he could.

I was really struck by a comment I heard from a speaker at an event in Ireland. 'If we all treated the world we live in with the greatest respect, and then handed it over to our children with the same instructions, in time people would be living in heaven on earth.'

I'd suggest keeping a lot of respect for the elderly in our society. They have in some way contributed to the life you have today. They deserve that acknowledgement. And remember, some say it will be you in their shoes.

"We make a living
by what we get,
we make a life
by what we give."

Winston Churchill.
Former British Prime Minister

WIIFM OR WIIFTW?

People who have changed the world are not always acknowledged in their lifetimes.

Unfortunately. Very often they can be out of step with the way the majority thinks. That's why they are seen as pioneers. And it's not until after they're gone that they get their recognition.

In the past, statues or plaques were erected to recognise the 'great'. Or they may have buildings named after them. Again, usually after they've died.

The actual reward for these people was in doing something they believed in, even when no-one believed in them.

Today's world has awards for many things. In the awards that mean something, the people who are honoured are the ones that have given of themselves to make a difference.

In a world that's often consumed with WIIFM (What's In It For Me?), you can distinguish yourself by focusing more on what you can give. I'd like to suggest an alternative. WIIFTW? What's In It For The World?

"Remember, if you ever need a helping hand, you'll find one at the end of your arm. . . . As you grow older you will discover that you have two hands. One for helping yourself, the other for helping others."

Audrey Hepburn
Actress, model and humanitarian
A beautiful woman in every way.

HELPING HAND

Yes, your hands are there to help yourself. And that is what many of us do.

This quote reminds us that it's not just about us. Everyone at some point needs help. Everyone.

It can be for different things. A flat tyre. Consolation after a relationship that's just ended. A loan of some money. Encouragement to start again.

When your life starts including the theme of helping others, then things start to get interesting.

And as a very wise man advised me, the ultimate charity is when you help someone and they don't know it was you. You get no recognition. You keep what you did secret. Nothing to feed your ego.

Very often some help others and their ego looks for the recognition that 'I helped you so I'm a good person.' A saint is one until they're told they're one. A true saint just does what they do because it's them. 'I helped you? I was only singing my own song.'

"I do think this next century, hopefully, will be about a more global view. Where you don't just think, yes my country is doing well, but you think about the world at large."

Bill Gates

Founder of Microsoft
Wealthiest Person in the world
according to Forbes, 2006.

YOUR WORLD

In Ireland, I'm always amazed at how vicious sports fans for clubs can be with each other. Yet, the same people who hate each other can sit beside one another cheering for their country. Then days later are back at each other's throats. I've never quite figured that one out. Bill Gates' comment to me hints at something similar. We can get very patriotic about our country yet not really care about the world our country is in.

Fundamentally, we are all from the same tribe. It might seem that you are from a different country, have a different religion or have a different coloured skin. But if you prick your finger, we all bleed the same colour blood.

There is a change coming. The world is starting to change. And it's coming from people who see the world as their home, not just their country. But more importantly, they see everyone on the planet as part of their family. With that kind of mindset, the effect on our world will be very different.

So, what about you? Are you taking a global view?

"Never doubt that a small group of thoughtful, committed citizens can change the world; indeed, it's the only thing that ever has."

Margaret Mead
1901-1978
Anthropologist

YOU CAN CHANGE THE WORLD

'What can I do? I'm only one against the might of governments. I can't change anything.'

Yes, you can. You don't have to be a world leader to change the world. All it takes is you making a difference where you are. If we all do that, then collectively it all adds up. Then change is inevitable. Everything you do make a difference in the bigger picture. Every stream flowing downhill eventually flows into a river and then into the sea.

Bob Geldof and his team forged the minds of 2 generations with Live Aid and Live 8. The courage and belief of one person can inspire people to do great things.

Everyone contributes to the well being of each other. The public, that is you, has more power than it thinks.

Governments realise this. Politicians realise this. That's why they pay attention to polls. And when the public fully realises the power it has, then things will really change. And it's starting.

INSPIRE ME

CHAPTER 15

SUCCESSFUL LIVING

Find your dream, then hold fast to it   309

Ask for advice from the best   311

The simplest success tool   313

Don't spend time doing this   315

Cultivate the art of appreciation   317

The way you think is vital   319

Anyone can be a leader   321

Dealing with obstacles.   323

Never continue in a job you don't enjoy   325

The key to a fulfilling life   327

"Champions aren't made in the gyms. Champions are made from something they have deep inside them - a desire, a dream, a vision."

Muhammad Ali

FIND YOUR DREAM, THEN HOLD FAST TO IT

Your dreams are clues to your destiny. They are what will inspire you to live a full and rewarding life. Muhammad Ali is giving a clue here as to what motivated him. He didn't just box and train hard in a gym only because he loved it.

No. He was motivated by his vision of the future. Of the benefits he would achieve by becoming world champion. Of the change he could affect in the world.

When you have a vision like this. It drives you out of bed in the morning. It keeps you going when a 'dull' day arrives. It literally gives you energy, even when your physical body is tired.

Spend time every week stoking the flames of your dreams. All of the people you know of, who have achieved something significant, all of them have had or have an inspiring dream.

If you don't have one, finding it starts with asking yourself a question. What is my life about? Keep asking it until you strike gold. It may take some time, but the reward is a life full of purpose and passion.

"Seek direction from one
who's already there."

Old Zulu Saying

ASK FOR ADVICE FROM THE BEST

Most things in life have been done by someone before you. Why bother making the same mistakes they made? Always seek advice from someone who has done it before you.

Want to write a book? Don't just speak to any author. Speak to someone who is very successful in the area you'd like to write in. Want to improve your health? Talk to someone who has transformed themselves or to someone who has proven they get great results.

And if it means paying for that information, then pay for it with a glad heart. Very often the cost of getting advice from someone experienced is worth more than the time or money wasted figuring out the same thing.

I remember being with a very talented friend who was speaking to someone in his industry. He asked the guy a lot of questions even though I thought my friend was more experienced.

Afterwards, I asked, 'Why did you not tell the guy how experienced you are?' He replied 'If I'd done that, then he wouldn't have told me everything he knew'.

"If we would only give,
just once, the same amount
of reflection to what we want
to get out of life that we give
to the question of what to do
with a two week vacation."

Dorothy Canfield Fisher
1879-1958
Educational reformer, social activist,
and best-selling American author

THE SIMPLEST SUCCESS TOOL

When you ask people about their holidays, you'll realise how much preparation they put into them.

They can spend days looking at brochures, websites and newspapers trying to find the best ways of getting the most from their time away. They'll ask people who've been there before.

They do this because they know that a bit of preparation and planning always makes a difference to the enjoyment of their holiday.

Yet, amazingly the same people will spend little to no time thinking or reflecting on their life. And the funny thing is that only a small amount of time yields amazing results. I've worked with many people on improving their lives. The most successful will always take some time out every week – somewhere they won't be interrupted – and reflect on the week just past, the week ahead and the bigger picture of their life.

Take time out to see what's working, what's not and what needs to be changed. This is so simple, that most people never do it. Will you?

"I am an old man
and have known a great
many troubles, but most of
them never happened."

Mark Twain

1835-1910

Humorist and Writer

DON'T SPEND
TIME ON THIS

Mr. Twain's remark is very sharp. We can spend countless hours lost in thoughts of worry, fear, doubt, concern and trouble. The reality is that it's mostly wasted time.

It's good to think things through. But it's not so good to strengthen the habit of worry. And that's all it is. A habit. But not a useful one.

Yes you will have challenges. And yes, you will get through them. But worrying about them before they happen is quite pointless. It doesn't make you feel good and if they never happen, what's the point in thinking of them?

Worry is just the habit of focusing on what you don't want to happen. Research has shown that happy people worry positively – that is they focus on what they want to happen.

And if as Mr. Twain says, most of what you picture doesn't happen anyway, it kind of makes sense to focus on the possible positive outcomes. At the very least, you'll feel better for having played happy pictures in your mind.

"Learn to enjoy every minute
of your life. Be happy now.
Don't wait for something
outside of yourself to make
you happy in the future.
Think how really precious is
the time you have to spend,
whether it's at work or with
your family. Every minute
should be enjoyed
and savoured."

Earl Nightingale
1921-1989
Radio Announcer, Author and Speaker

CULTIVATE THE ART OF APPRECIATION

If you speak with anyone who enjoys life, you will be struck by how much they enjoy it.

They appreciate everything and not to a silly degree. They just have an air of thankfulness for all they have, even if to you, it's very little.

We can fall into the trap of 'when I get this…then I'll be happy'. Forget about what's to come. What is in your life to appreciate now?

Great friends? Loved ones? Your health?

None of us know when our time will come to leave the earth. It'd be nice to think we had some enjoyment before we left!

Oprah Winfrey has a simple way of bringing more appreciation into your life. Get a note book and every night write down six things you are thankful for.

This might sound silly, but it focuses your mind on what's good and bright in your life. And no matter what your situation, there is always something to appreciate.

"The significant problems we
face cannot be solved at the
same level of thinking we were
at when we created them."

Albert Einstein

A pretty smart guy.

CHANGE THE WAY YOU THINK

Mr. Einstein says something here that is so simple it will probably be missed by most.

What he's saying is that for the big challenges we face in life (the ones we very often cause), we need to change our mindset towards it and come at it from a different perspective.

We almost need to imagine that we've solved the problem, and then look at it through those eyes.

It brings a very different perspective and encourages fresh thinking. In fact, if you can learn to do that and think in terms of solving issues as opposed to 'I have a big problem', you'll be shocked (not just surprised) at how quickly things can change.

And I think Mr. Einstein knows what he's talking about. Like the Apple ad's go…'Think different.'

"Leaders are not born; they are made. And they are made just like anything else - through hard work. And that is the price we'll have to pay to achieve any goal."

Vince Lombardi

Hall of Fame American Football Coach

Anyone Can Be A Leader

It's not easy being a good leader.

That is, someone who inspires others to be better. To generate belief and confidence in you, so that others follow you towards a brighter future. To pioneer change in a world that likes the 'norm'.

The key here is that leadership can be learned. And for the future it is vital as a skill. For sport, for business, for communities and for families.

We learn through training, through experience and through application. Too many leaving school today assume they will automatically be leaders in the modern world.

They may well be great leaders in time but they will have had to practice the art of leadership and in the process have made a lot of mistakes.

The skill of leading and managing people is a craft. Like all crafts it takes time, dedication and a reason for doing it. The key is to start being a leader to yourself.

"Obstacles don't have to stop you. If you run into a wall, don't turn around and give up. Figure out how to climb it, go through it, or work around it."

Michael Jordan

One of the greatest basketball players ever

Dealing With Obstacles

The clearer you are on what you want. The less you'll be hindered by obstacles. It's not that they go away. No, no. It's more that they just become things to overcome. Everyone who has achieved anything significant has often overcome what seemed insurmountable obstacles.

The majority stop at the first hurdle. The minority keep going until they find a way around it. That's largely because they have a clear picture of what they want and very importantly why they want it. (Their why is the driving force.)

When you want something badly enough, you'll do anything to get it. And that's an important factor. You have to really, really, really want it. When you're clear on your goal, and your motivation, obstacles become a means to get closer to your objective. Persistence is one of the key elements in success and Michael Jordan had it in buckets.

And even when he became recognised as great, he was usually the last one off the practice ground. Obstacles don't last long with someone who has that level of commitment.

"Never continue in a job you don't enjoy. If you're happy in what you're doing, you'll like yourself, you'll have inner peace. And if you have that, along with physical health, you will have had more success than you could possibly have imagined."

Johnny Carson
1925-2005
Talk Show Host and Entertainer

NEVER CONTINUE IN A JOB YOU DON'T ENJOY...

Or maybe you can change the job you're in to make it more enjoyable. Maybe you can change your attitude towards it. (Because a lot of people have the wrong attitude towards their work)

But if, after doing the above you still don't enjoy what you're doing, then find something you do and move. Take the risk and go.

When you work on something you love, you have one of life's greatest gifts. And yes, it is possible to work at what you love AND make money.

Why? Because enjoyment at work is a result of passion in what you do. I've worked with many people who have changed careers to do what they love. Sometimes they make more money, sometimes they make a bit less. But what increases all the time is their wealth.

That is wealth, as measured by happiness, good health and a more balanced life. Plus their self-esteem rockets because they usually end up doing something that fits with them as a person. And that is priceless.

"Don't spend your precious
time asking 'Why isn't the
world a better place?'
It will only be time wasted.
The question to ask is
'How can I make it better?'
To that there is an answer."

Leo Buscaglia

Author and Speaker

THE KEY TO A FULFILLING LIFE

Quality of life is inside-out. The greatest fulfilment you can experience is in reaching out and helping others. In living for something bigger than you.

Unfortunately, most people think that when 'I succeed materially, I'll be fulfilled.' But that never happens, particularly if their success is based on getting something. All they get is an empty feeling. A hollowness. A knowing that there is more to life.

All of the wisdom literature down through the ages agrees on this point. You increase your level of fulfilment by improving the quality of life of others. And the great thing is that this can be done in many different ways.

It usually doesn't involve you giving money to charity (even though that is worthy). Fulfilment usually comes from giving your most valuable commodity. Time. So like the quote opposite says, don't be one who gives out about the world. Be one who has made the decision to make it better. To start, just ask yourself how.

SHANE CRADOCK

Shane Cradock is a leading business and performance expert in helping individuals and organisations to prosper.

He has over 20 years experience working across 50 industries and his clients include successful entrepreneurs, Top 10 Fortune executives, household brand names and ambitious sports people. They are all hungry for personal and career growth - but in a way that enhances their quality of life.

A speaker to audiences from all walks of life, he suffered a severe personal breakdown in his mid-twenties. Coming through that challenging time gave him a different insight into how to really thrive. As a result, he puts a massive emphasis on the 'inner game' and has transformed people's lives through his work.

His home is in Ireland, and he is originally from the great hurling county of Kilkenny. He now lives with his wife Judy and his children, Jane and Sam, in the beautiful county of Wicklow - nicknamed the 'garden of Ireland'. (Sparky the dog, gets a look in too.)

An award winning playwright, every Monday, he writes a short inspirational email that goes out to people all over the world.

You can find out more information about Shane and his work at www.shanecradock.com

Printed in Great Britain
by Amazon